Hanban / Confucius Institute Headquarters

DISCOVER CHINA

China Intercontinental Press

Discover China

Publisher	Lin Xu
Publishing Senior Supervisor	Jianfei Ma
Publishing Supervisor	Wenzheng Sun
	Jinhong Wang
	Wuhan Lin
Chief Editor	Linda Asare Annan (USA)
	Wen Ruan
Editor	Keyhan Jethani (India)
	Philip Tesoriero (USA)
	Gulai Wang
Editor-in-charge	Xiaomin Jing
	Lei Zheng
Art Director	Zhijie Yan
Art Design	Peng Liu
Graph Drawing	Jingyi Xie
Photo	Weidong Wu
	Guodong Li
	Ling Jiang
	Ying Tang
	CFP
	FOTOE
	TEMPO ARTS

CONTENTS

FOREWORD

*D*iscover *China*, a book for readers around the world, can also be a popular learning aid for people who are interested in Chinese culture. This book can be a supplement any reading material that requires little or no tutor supervision as its content facilitates independent reading.

This book provides a variety of information about China, ranging from Chinese history, geography to her economy and education. From traditional festivals to modern living, beautiful sceneries and unique local cuisines, the informative nature of this book presents a traditional yet modern China to its readers.

This book is filled with 100 interesting subjects, each visually demonstrated with appropriate Chinese elements. There are also over 200 appealing pictures to stimulate an imaginative learning process and actively engage our readers. We know this book can become a window to understand China, and the bridge for learning Chinese culture.

We are deeply grateful for the support from Hanban/Confucius Institute Headquarters, and the experts from home and abroad for providing us with great suggestions in the compilation of this book.

The Editorial Committee
September 2009

Geography of China

China, an ancient, mysterious and beautiful land, is the third largest country in the world. It occupies an area of 3,705,407 square miles, and spans 62 degrees of longitude and 49 degrees of latitude. Its numerous natural wonders span a variety of climates and terrains, from soaring, snow-capped mountains to warm, resplendent seas. Abundant in a variety of resources, plants, animals and minerals, the land has nurtured countless generations of Chinese people.

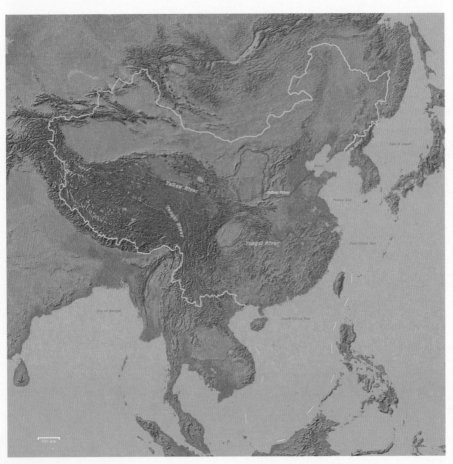

Geographic map of China

A map of China

China is located in the eastern part of the Asian continent, on the western Pacific Rim. China is slightly larger than the United States. It's approximately seventeen times the size of France, about 386,000 square miles smaller than all of Europe, and 231,661 square miles smaller than Oceania (Australia, New Zealand, and the islands of the south and central Pacific). Additional offshore territory, including territorial waters, special economic areas, and the continental shelf, totals over 1.1 million square miles, bringing China's overall territory to over 3.7 million square miles.

Western China's Himalayan Mountains are often referred to as the roof of the world. Mount Qomolangma (known to the West as Mount Everest), is the peak, at over 29,000 feet in height. China stretches from its westernmost point on the Pamir Plateau to the confluence of the Heilongjiang and Wusuli Rivers, 3,231 miles to the east.

Satellite view of Earth

When inhabitants of eastern China are greeting the dawn, people in western China still face four more hours of darkness. The distance from northernmost point in China to the southernmost point is approximately 3,400 miles. When northern China is still gripped in a world of ice and snow, flowers are already blooming in the balmy south. China's maritime territory includes 5,400 islands, which have a total area of 30,888 square miles. The two largest islands, Taiwan and Hainan, cover 13,899 square miles and 13,127 square miles respectively.

China possesses 12,427 miles of land border, plus 11,184 miles of coastline. Setting out from any point on China's border and making a complete circuit back to the starting point, the distance traveled would be equivalent to circling the globe at the equator.

Due to its vast area, China experiences a range of climates. Temperature belts from south to north appear in this order: tropical zone, subtropical zone, temperate zone, medium temperate zone and frigid temperate zone. There is also a vertical climatic zone on the Qinghai-Tibet Plateau in southwestern China.

002

Beijing

If you choose to visit only one city in China, it should definitely be Beijing. It is endowed with numerous world-famous attractions, which are renowned far beyond China's borders. It is not only a city with splendid history, but also a modern, international city. It not only has a wealth of sights and artifacts from the imperial courts and nobility, but also contains many examples of folk art forms. And, it is not just famous for its cultural heritage - it is an emerging destination for prestigious international business meetings.

This city enjoys a long and interesting history, which is readily apparent in the many historic and cultural attractions. Beijing's lengthy and illustrious history started some 500,000 years ago. It is here that the ancestors of modern Homo sapiens, Peking men, lived in caves. Records show that Beijing has been an inhabited city for more than 3,000 years, and has endured invasions by warlords and foreign powers, devastating fires, the rise and fall of powerful imperial dynasties. Yet, despite its long history

Tian'anmen Rostrum

of trials and tribulations, Beijing emerges each time from its troubles as a strong and vibrant city.

For more than 800 years - from the Yuan Dynasty (1271—1368) to the Ming (1368—1644) and Qing (1644—1911) dynasties - Beijing was a capital city. Thirty-four emperors have lived in and ruled the nation from Beijing, and it has been an important trading city from its earliest days.

It certainly contains a plethora of world-famous tourist sites. For example, the Forbidden City is the largest and best-preserved imperial palace complex in the world. Tian'anmen Square is the biggest central square in the world. The Temple of Heaven is the largest sacrificial complex in the world. And, the Great Wall is one of the great wonders in the world.

Tourists may find it a charming place that combines modernity and history. Guests will surely be impressed by the integration of traditional culture and breakneck modernization that has taken the grip of the city - traditional Hutong courtyard complexes stand next to impressive skyscrapers.

Beijing is a hub of communications, with good railroad and air links to all parts of China, as well as many major cities all over the world, thus facilitating the rapid development of tourism as an important industry in Beijing. Today, Beijing is becoming a sparkling metropolis with modern

The Hall of Prayer for Good Harvests, Temple of Heaven

skyscrapers, museums, art galleries, shopping malls, efficient transportation and numerous foreign investment enterprises. The 2008 Beijing Olympic Games introduced it as a fashionable, dynamic, modern, and also ·grand and mysterious capital to people all over world.

Refurbished Qianmen shopping street

Strolling around Beijing today, you'll find it has much in common with any other great metropolis elsewhere. There are towering skyscrapers, busy shopping malls and an endless stream of traffic that makes the city much the same as others. The most famous and popular commercial plazas and pedestrian shopping streets are predominantly located near the Yansha Shopping Mall, Tian'anmen and Wangfujing Street, Guomao Shopping Mall, Qianmen Street and Xidan Street. However, although you will find multinational chains familiar from back home, nowhere else on earth will you find such a variety of gourmet Chinese restaurants offering the very best of the eight different styles of Chinese cuisine, as well as Western-style dishes. Modern hotels abound, each offering the highest standards of service and convenience.

After a day filled with Beijing tours, nighttime can hold other surprises for you. Nightlife varies widely, from traditional performances such as the Peking Opera, acrobatics and martial arts, to rock concerts, ballroom dancing and bars and clubs. Each and every one has its own unique flavor, and there is something for everyone in Beijing. Everywhere you will encounter smiling faces and a warm welcome, especially from the children who love to say hello. All these things add up to truly make your visit the cultural experience of a lifetime.

003

Shanghai

Unlike many tourist cities in China, Shanghai is impressive because of its relatively short history - less than 200 years. However, Shanghai witnessed the most important period of history of modern China. As a young city, it serves as an open door from China to the outside world. It always follows the newest, cutting-edge trends in business and leisure, and provides a window for the Chinese to learn about new developments overseas.

Shanghai is located in China's central eastern coast near the mouth of Yangtze River. Ever since 19th century, it has flourished as a bustling port between East and West. Today, it still plays an important role in the mainland shipping and cargo industry, and is one of the busiest and largest ports in the world.

Today, Shanghai is a world-renowned metropolis. It is hard to imagine it was still a fishing and textiles village in 19th century. Having suffered the ravages of wars, social turmoil and economic crisis, Shanghai has kept its sights firmly fixed in the future, and has seen its fortunes rise exponentially due to the economic reforms of the past forty years. Now, it is one of the most busy economic centers in the world, and more than

Night view of the Bund

Shikumen

300 of the world's top 500 enterprises have established branches or are developing centers here.

Foreigners will find traveling here easy and enjoyable, because many foreigners work and live in Shanghai, it is a very friendly city to visitors. Its rapid progress made it a miracle for Chinese people and the world. In the eyes of many Westerners, Shanghai is a fantastic place that displays the essence of modern China. In Chinese people's eyes, Shanghai is an excellent city that blends the elements of East and West, displaying the most modern technology and fresh trends, while still preserving its unique Chinese heritage.

On one side of town hundreds of skyscrapers dominate the most prosperous streets and make it no different from New York or London, yet on the other side of town traditional homes, called "shikumen", are scattered in corners and hidden in the twisting, narrow alleys of some of Shanghai's older districts. Shanghai has many attractions in the downtown area, including Huangpu River, the Bund, Oriental Pearl TV Tower, Jinmao Tower, Shanghai Museum, Yuyuan Garden, Xintiandi and the special old streets and lanes.

View from the Bund - Lujiazui Financial District

Shanghai is also said to be a shopper's paradise. Almost every famous international brand is on display in the bustling commercial streets like Nanjing Road, Huaihai Road and North Sichuan Road. Today it attracts more and more international fashion shows and other cultural shows - it is known as the fashion capital of China.

Visitors who love to eat cannot miss Shanghai cuisine, which belongs to one of the eight schools of Chinese cuisine. It is famous for the delicacy and exquisiteness of its flavors, and complexity of its cooking techniques.

004

Chongqing

When talking about Chongqing, the first deep impression would be its large size. As one of the four municipalities in China, the other three are Beijing, Shanghai and Tianjin, it is also the largest city in western China. Located on the edge of the Yungui Plateau, Chongqing is crossed by the Jialing River and the upper reaches of the Yangtze River. It contains Daba Shan Mountain in the north, Wu Shan Mountain in the east, Wuling Shan Mountain in the southeast, and Dalou Mountain to the south.

Chongqing has a humid subtropical climate, with the two-season monsoonal variations typical of South Asia. As one of the "Three Furnaces" (三大火炉), Chongqing's summers are among the hottest in China. The temperature can be as high as 43℃, with an average high of 35℃ in August. Yet even in the hottest weather the wind is often cold,

The fog capital - Chongqing

The city built against hills and waters

making high temperatures more bearable. Winters are fairly mild, but damp and overcast; average January highs are 9℃. Chongqing has one of the lowest sunshine totals annually in China. With the weather at its best in the spring and fall, these are the best times to visit the city of Chongqing.

Chongqing can get foggy sometimes, and suffers from heavy air pollution. Chongqing is famous for its foggy weather in spring and winter days, which gives this city a nickname of 雾都, in English "the Fog Capital". The city government has been aggressively trying to improve its air quality in recent years.

Chongqing attracts visitors from home and abroad for its cultural heritage and other tourist attractions. The city is the starting point for the Yangtze River Cruise, which explores the stunning scenery of the Three Gorges. Other attractions include the Dazu Rock Carvings, valuable works of art carved during the 9th Century, Gold Buddhist Mountain,

Chongqing night view

a rich repository of diverse animals and plants; and Fishing Town, one of three ancient battlefields in China. Ancient Ci Qi Kou village lures tourists to linger in its streets to buy handicraft souvenirs.

Chongqing is famous for its hot Sichuan cuisine and world-famous hotpot dishes. Street vendors as well as restaurants feature exciting spicy delicacies for the adventurers.

Chongqing local cuisine

Harbin

The ice and snow are Harbin's greatest attraction. Multicolored ice lanterns, vivid ice and snow carvings and exciting ice sports will be sure to bring you lots of fun. Located on the bank of Songhua River, Harbin is the capital and largest city of Heilongjiang Province, northeastern China. The average temperature in summer is 21.2℃, -16.8℃ in winter. It can be as cold as -38.1℃ in winter. Thus it is reputed as the "Ice City". Each winter fantastic sculptures created from snow and ice, ice lanterns and exciting sporting events attract thousands of visitors from China and abroad. The cool summers make Harbin highly popular as a natural summer resort.

Often nicknamed as "Oriental Moscow" or "Oriental Paris" for the Western architecture of its downtown, Harbin grew with the arrival of the far-east railway, constructed by the Russians in the late 19th century. It used to be a place for lots of white refugees, who left behind a few

Colorful ice lanterns in Harbin International Ice and Snow Festival

St. Sophia Cathedral

A snow sculpture

Western style buildings of Gothic, Baroque and Byzantine styles built by the Russians and other Europeans.

It is also becoming the center for winter activities like skiing, skating, winter-swimming, and watching ice lanterns and ice sculptures. Every year since 1985 starting from January 5 and lasting for one month, is Harbin's Ice and Snow Festival, lots of celebrations will be held during the period. Many tourists from China and abroad come to visit this legendary "Ice City". Now the Harbin International Ice and Snow Festival has become one of the world's four largest ice and snow festivals, along with Japan's Sapporo Snow Festival, Canada's Quebec City Winter Carnival, and Norway's Ski Festival.

006

Kunming

This city is a must for tourists coming to China. Not only does it provide historical sites and cultural relics, but it is also a city where spring seems to last forever. The "spring city" has flowers that blossom all year round making a walk through the city an enjoyable pastime. Not to mention the clean air has a hint of the flowery smell wafting in it.

The Grand View Tower is a three story square building. It houses a 180 character long couplet which is honored as the longest couplet in ancient and modern times. On top of the cultural aspect of the site, tourists can have an amazing panoramic view of the area. They will be touched by the mountains that surround them and the lake that rests besides the tower. You will feel completely relaxed as you witness the boundless sky with the sun shining brightly to reflect on the glassy surface of the lake.

Stone Forest

The Grand View Tower

Seagulls on the Lake Dianchi

The Kunming International Horticultural Expo Site is also a must for any fan of gardening. The humongous area holds many buildings that contain the wonders of Chinese gardening. One can't help but be stunned by the wide array of flowers and other types of fauna that exist in China. The hugely successful 1999 International Horticultural Exposition enhanced Kunming's influence in the world resulting in a snowball effect upon tourism as more and more foreigners come to discover this enchanting part of China.

Kunming is the focal point of Yunnan minority culture. Some 26 ethnic minorities such as Yi, Bai, Miao, Dai, Hani inhabit the region. Each group has its own featured festivals such as the Torch festival of Yi people, the Golden Temple Fair and so on.

Its alluring highland scenery, bewitching karst topography, varied and exotic habitats and customs and places of historical interest can be found at major scenic spots such as Dianchi Lake, Stone Forest, the Village of Ethnic Culture, and the Grand View Pavilion.

Lastly, do not forget to buy some locally produced souvenirs for your friends or family when you visit Kunming, such as ivory or wood carvings, and minority-produced tie dyed items. You will find a variety of stores to meet your every desire.

007

Jiuzhaigou Valley

It is said to be a fairyland on the earth because no elsewhere could have such stunning scenery in every season. Jiuzhaigou Valley is a natural reserve in the north of Sichuan. Its name is due to the existence of nine stockade villages of Tibetan origin, and it is regarded as a holy mountain and watercourse by the Tibetan people.

With an average elevation of 2000 m, it is bounded with exotic attractions and dreamlike scenery. Crystal clear lakes, colorful pools, waterfalls, verdant forests, majestic snow-covered mountains and rare species are all here.

In the valley, there is a pond that is known as the "Five Color Pond" which is must-see scenery in summer. This mystical pond actually is called five-colored because it reflects the colors of the leaves in its waters. It is amazing sight - the water has a mirror-like image of the trees floating on its surface. When you walk around the pond, the trees set off a wonderful image of a wonderland. The colors of the leaves seem painted on with

Jiuzhaigou Valley

Waterfall in Jiuzhaigou Valley

a magic brush. The colors are so vibrant and radiant that it seems surreal. Maybe fairies live in the trees, giving them their beautiful glow. While looking into the water, you will get an urge to go swimming. The water is so refreshing, it will cool you to the core.

Jiuzhaigou Valley

Another famous attraction is Nuorilang Waterfall which is 32 meters (about 105 feet) wide and 25 meters (about 82 feet) tall. Nuorilang means "grand and magnificent" in Tibetan, and it is indeed a gorgeous waterfall. The top of the waterfall is very flat. It is said that originally there was no waterfall, but a platform here long ago. Then a monk brought a spinning wheel when he returned to this place. A Tibetan girl learned the skill of spinning, so she carried the wheel to the platform and showed her sisters how to spin. A cruel man, Roza, thought that she was doing something evil and kicked her and the spinning wheel off the cliff. In no time, torrents rushed Roza and his accomplices down the mountain, so the platform turned into the waterfall. When the sun shines in the morning, flowery rainbows can be seen in the sky, which make the waterfall more charming and splendid.

When visitors come in winter, the majestic snowcapped mountaintops will leave you in such a peaceful and silent surrounding. The white colored mountaintops create a beautiful contrast against the baby blue sky. Along the trails, you can see the many waterfalls that are hidden within the valley. The waterfall splits into many different parts as the water pours over the protruding rocks. The water cascading over the rocks is like a white veil. When you stand a bit farther away, the whole picture is amazing. The sight of the separate miniature waterfalls look like the scales of an immense white dragon.

008

Museum of Qin Terra Cotta Warriors and Horses

The Qin Terra Cotta Figures, life-sized sculpted warriors and horses arranged in battle formations, are the most significant archeological excavation of the 20th century. They are replicas of what the imperial guard would have looked like in ancient times. Work is ongoing at this site, which is around 1.5 kilometers east of Emperor Qin Shi Huang's Mausoleum, Lintong County, Shaanxi Province. It is a sight not to be missed by any visitor to China. Xi'an and the Museum of Qin Terra Cotta Warriors and Horses have become landmarks on all travelers' itinerary.

Upon ascending the throne at the age of 13 (in 246 BC), Qin Shi Huang, later the first Emperor of unified China, had begun to work for his mausoleum. It took 11 years to finish. It is speculated that many

No. 2 pit of Qin Terra Cotta Warriors and Horses Museum

buried treasures and sacrificial objects had accompanied the emperor in his afterlife. The terra cotta soldiers were discovered when a group of peasants uncovered some pottery while digging for a well nearby the royal tomb in 1974. It caught the attention of archeologists immediately. They came to Xi'an in droves to study and to extend

Qin Terra Cotta Warriors and Horses

the digs. They have established beyond doubt that these artifacts were associated with the Qin Dynasty (211-206 BC).

The museum is divided into three sections: No. 1 Pit, No. 2 Pit, and No. 3 Pit respectively. They were tagged in the order of their discoveries. No. 1 Pit is the largest, and first opened to the public on China's National Day, 1979. There are columns of soldiers at the front, followed by war chariots at the back. No. 2 Pit, found in 1976, is 20 meters northeast of No. 1 Pit. It contained over a thousand warriors and 90 chariots of wood. It was unveiled to the public in 1994. Archeologists came upon No. 3 Pit also in 1976, 25 meters northwest of No. 1 Pit. It looked like the command center of the armed forces. It went on display in 1989, with 68 warriors, a war chariot and four horses.

Altogether over 7,000 pottery soldiers, horses, chariots, and weapons have been unearthed from these pits. Most of them have been restored to their former grandeur. The Terra Cotta Warriors and Horses is a sensational archeological find. It has put Xi'an on the map for tourists. It was listed by UNESCO in 1987 as one of the world cultural heritage sites.

009

Fujian Earthen Houses

Fujian Earthen house (Tulou in Chinese) is a unique Chinese rammed earth building made by the Hakka and other people in the mountainous areas of southwestern Fujian, China. Nestled in the mountainous and wild lands of Fujian, Tulou are communal houses built for protection against bandits and wild animals. Built from the 11th to the 20th Century in the mountainous areas across Fujian and neighboring provinces, the Tulou buildings could house an entire clan.

Strong outer walls surround the Tulou's inner halls, storehouses, wells and bedrooms, functioning almost as a small, fortified city. The houses were made of earth, stone, bamboo and wood, which are all readily available materials. After constructing the walls with rammed earth, branches, strips of wood and bamboo chips were laid in the wall as a skeleton to reinforce it. The end result is a well-lit, well-ventilated, windproof, earthquake-proof building that is warm in winter and cool in summer.

They are three to five stories high and usually house dozens of families. They are usually enclosed and can be square, circular or oval-shaped, all with a thick earth wall reinforced with wood. They have only one entrance that is protected by thick wooden doors reinforced with an outer shell of iron. The top level of the earth buildings has gun holes for defense against bandits.

The foundations of Tulou buildings were built with paving stones on top of compacted earth, in two to three tiers. There is a circular drain around the top tier of the foundation to prevent rainwater from damaging the Tulou's wall.

Yongding Tulou inside

Tulou complex

Over 20,000 of these houses still stand today, ten of which are over 600 years old. The oldest one, "Fu Xing Lou" was constructed over 1,200 years ago and is regarded as a "living fossil" of the construction style of central China.

The Tulou located at the border of Yongding County and Nanjing County - the most prolific area for Tulou houses - is the perfect example of this style of construction. Most of the well-recognized Tulou buildings are located in this area. One Tulou in Yongding County has 384 rooms and once housed more than 800 people.

Forty-six Tulous were declared in 2008 by UNESCO as World Heritage Sites, "as exceptional examples of a building tradition and function exemplifying a particular type of communal living and defensive organization, and, in terms of their harmonious relationship with their environment," they were found to be exceptional.

010

Beijing's Compound Courtyard

The courtyard, a traditional unique home, has a long history in Chinese architecture. These homes, which are tucked into Beijing's Hutong - narrow alleyways of homes - represent a rich tradition. Courtyard homes are called "Siheyuan" in Chinese, "Si" means four, which here refers to the four directions: north, south, east and west. "He" means surrounding, referring to the four walls that surround the square inner courtyard of the home. Yuan means "courtyard", which is the common area in the center of a "Siheyuan".

A typical Siheyuan layout at No.67 Dongsi Jiutiao, Dongcheng district, Beijing

Due to its special layout, you can think of the Siheyuan as a box with a garden in the center. There is only one gate leading to a Hutong, so when the gate is closed the courtyard loses touch with the outside world. In this peaceful space, family members can fully enjoy tranquility and share the happiness of domestic life.

The gate of a traditional Siheyuan decorated with stone lion

The Siheyuan is a typical form of ancient Chinese architecture, especially in the north of China. They are designed to make living in a climate that is sometimes inhospitable as comfortable as possible. For instance, the Siheyuan is enclosed and inward-facing to protect them from the harsh winter winds and the dust storms of spring. Their design also reflects the traditions of China, following the rules of Feng Shui and the patriarchal, Confucian tenants of order and hierarchy that have been so important to society.

Most of the existing courtyards are relics of the Ming (1368—1644) and Qing (1644—1911) Dynasties. Their ancient furniture, tranquil fish ponds, wooden doors and windows, and cane chairs remind you of their flourishing past. Their intricate Chinese eaves, fine brick designs, and wooden carvings reveal the strong classical tone of old Beijing. Hidden in a forest of armored concrete, the Siheyuan presents an aching beauty of past luxury, waiting eagerly for you to explore the past. You cannot fully understand Beijing until you have lived in a courtyard home.

Owners of the courtyards often plant flowers and trees in their garden, growing their own cheerful Garden of Eden. Generally speaking, they love planting date trees, locust trees and cloves. The pomegranate tree is also a favorite because it has many seeds.In Chinese, the pronunciations of "seed" and "son" are the same, and the elderly believe that the more sons you have, the more blessings you receive. This is the reason we can see many

A Siheyuan garden

pomegranate trees growing in courtyard homes. Living in this elegant and harmonious environment, many enjoy a peaceful and blissful life!

The Hutong and the courtyards reflect the ritualistic and traditional ideas of China, and contain rich cultural connotations. They are the archetypes of the royal architecture. Unfortunately, these traditional dwellings, rich in heritage, are being replaced by high-rise buildings during the remodeling and reconstruction of the city. People in China and abroad are concerned that the historic and cultural value of Beijing will be deminished if the Hutong and courtyards are destroyed and lost forever.

Qiao's Compound

U nder the influence of Confucianism, ancient Chinese people strictly conformed to "filial piety" which demands that children take care of their parents and live with them. As a result, grandparents, parents, children and grandchildren lived together under the same roof generation after generation. That's why some of the houses belonging to one family are very big. The famous Qiao's Compound is just such a case.

As another masterpiece of traditional civil architecture in Northern China, Qiao's Compound lies at Qiaojiapu Village, about 35 miles south of Taiyuan. It was the residential house of the well-known financier Qiao Zhiyong of the Qing Dynasty. First built in 1756, and renovated and expanded later, this compound has been turned into a magnificent complex with the unique character of traditional architecture.

Part of Qiao's Compound

The Qiao's Compound spreads out over two acres of land, consisting of six large yards and 20 small yards with 313 rooms in total. It was an old Chinese residential courtyard that thrived for over two centuries.

Entering the gate of the courtyard, you will see an 260-foot-long straight stone walkway that divides the six courtyards into two parts. There are sloped protections between the pavements and nearby walls.

At the end of the western side stands the Qiao family's ancestral temple, which contains four main buildings and six other structures. The sidewalks on the roof of every courtyard are connected to allow for patrolling. Viewed from outside, the residence is solemn and grand; viewed from inside, it is splendid and orderly, reflecting the residential style of big families in feudal society in Northern China.

One of the courtyards in Qiao's Compound

Brick carvings can be seen everywhere in the yards. Backbone carvings, wall carvings, and railing carvings, all of which are based on folk figures, literary allusions, flowers and plants, birds, beasts, chess, painting and calligraphy. The carving designs are so exquisite and their workmanship fine, fully showing the special style of residential building in the Qing Dynasty.

In 1990, this ancient mansion became more famous all over China and abroad

The red lanterns hanging outside the gate

thanks to the movie Raise the Red Lantern by the director Zhang Yimou. After the filming was finished, the drama production team left behind several hundred red lanterns. Since then, these lanterns have been the most important decoration both in the Qiao Family Grand Courtyard and other Jin Merchants courtyards.

012

The Grand Canal of China

The Grand Canal of China, also known as the Beijing-Hangzhou Grand Canal, is the longest ancient canal or manmade waterway in the world with a total length of 1,770 km (1,114 miles). The canal connects the present cities of Beijing in the north and Hangzhou in the south, contains 24 locks and 60 bridges. Since most of China's major rivers flow from west to east, the fact that the Grand Canal runs north and south provides an important connector between the Yangtze River valley and the Yellow River valley, and other minor river systems.

The series of waterways in eastern China is long and old, which makes the Grand Canal a masterpiece of ancient times. The oldest section between the Yangtze River and the Yellow River was constructed during the 4th and 5th centuries B.C.

The canal we see today was built section by section in different areas and dynasties before it was linked together by the 6th Century. In

Gongchen Bridge on the Grand Canal in Hangzhou

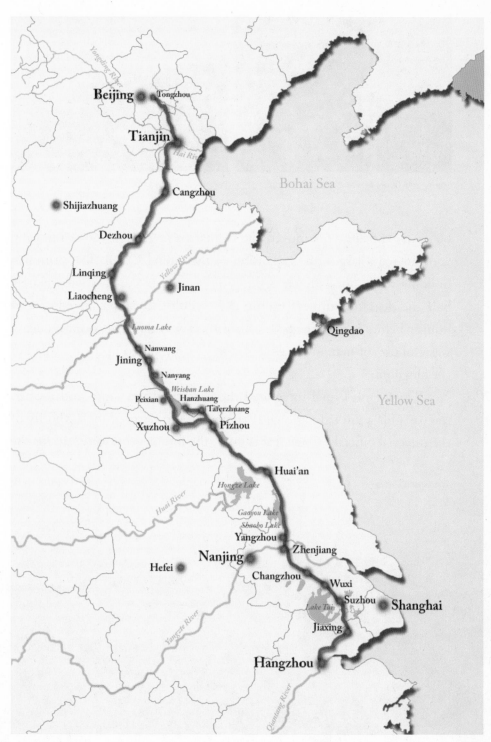

A map of the Grand Canal

The Grand Canal in Hangzhou, Zhejiang   Part of the Grand Canal

605 AD, the emperor moved the capital from Hangzhou to Luoyang and ordered a large-scale expansion of the Grand Canal. The primitive building techniques stretched the project over six years. Approximately half the peasant builders (about 3,000,000) died of hard labor and hunger before it was finished. This project was thought to have been a wasteful use of manpower and money, which resulted in the downfall of the kingdom.

The Grand Canal integrated the north and the south and formed the basis for a unified national economy. It also restored the authority of the imperial officials. Once it was built, the foundations were laid for the

The Grand Canal

Part of the Grand Canal   The Grand Canal in Huai'an, Jiangsu

brilliant epoch of the Tang Dynasty (618-907), as China emerged as the most powerful state in the world.

As a major transportation hinge in past dynasties, the Grand Canal interconnected the Yangtze, Yellow, Huai, and Qiantang Rivers and flowed through Beijing, Tianjin, Hebei, Shandong, Jiangsu and Zhejiang with Hangzhou at its southernmost end. The Grand Canal, which joined the river systems from different directions, offered much facility to transport foods and goods from south to north in past times. It greatly improved the administration and defense of China as a whole and strengthened economic and cultural intercourse between north and south.

Boating on this ancient Chinese canal is one of the best ways to get a panoramic view of the landscape of typical river towns in southern China, which includes ancient dwellings, stone bridges of traditional designs and historical relics. Experiencing some of the local customs offers much delight to travelers. Tourists also have an opportunity to enjoy good food while appreciating the surrounding scenery.

013

History of China

China is one of the longest, single, unified civilizations in the world. In ancient mythology, Chinese civilization began with Pangu, the creator of the universe, and progressed as other legendary heroes taught people to use fire, make clothing, build shelters and communicate.

As early as 5,000 to 6,000 years ago, people in the Yellow River valley had already started farming and raising livestock. The first prehistoric dynasty was the Xia, which existed from about 2100 to 1600 B.C. The Xia Dynasty fell between the late Neolithic age and the Bronze Age. The Shang Dynasty started around 1600 B.C. It was then that people learned how to smelt bronze and use iron tools. White pottery and glazed pottery were also produced. Silk production was well developed, and the world's first figured inlaid silk weaving technique was being used. During the Spring and Autumn Period (722-476 B.C.), steel production technologies appeared.

The ever prosperous silk road still attracts many tourists

The Qin Dynasty was founded by Qin Shi Huang, in 221 B.C. Qin Shi Huang, a man of great talent and bold vision, ended the rivalry among the independent principalities of the Warring States Period, and established the first centralized, unified, multi-ethnic state in Chinese history. During his reign, Qin Shi Huang standardized the writing language, currencies, weights and measures, established the system of prefectures and

Chime-bell

counties, and constructed the world-renowned Great Wall and his legendary mausoleum. Today, the thousands of life-size terracotta horses and armored warriors that guard Qin Shi Huang's tomb in Xi'an attract swarms of Chinese and foreign visitors every day.

Chronology of dynasties

Dynasty			Years
Three Sovereigns and Five Emperors	三皇五帝	sān huáng wǔ dì	before 2070 BCE
Xia Dynasty	夏	xià	2100 BCE - 1600 BCE
Shang Dynasty	商	shāng	1600 BCE - 1046 BCE
Western Zhou Dynasty	西周	xī zhōu	1046 BCE - 771 BCE
Eastern Zhou Dynasty	东周	dōng zhōu	770 BCE - 256 BCE
Traditionally divided into Spring and Autumn Period	春秋	chūn qiū	722 BCE - 476 BCE
Warring States Period	战国	zhàn guó	475 BCE - 221 BCE
Qin Dynasty	秦	qín	221 BCE - 206 BCE
Western Han Dynasty	西汉	xī hàn	206 BCE - 9 CE
Xin Dynasty	新	xīn	9 - 23
Eastern Han Dynasty	东汉	dōng hàn	25 - 220
Three Kingdoms	三国	sān guó	220 - 265
Western Jin Dynasty	西晋	xī jìn	265 - 317
Eastern Jin Dynasty	东晋	dōng jìn	317 - 420
Southern and Northern Dynasties	南北朝	nán běi cháo	420 - 589
Sui Dynasty	隋	suí	581 - 618
Tang Dynasty	唐	táng	618 - 907
Five Dynasties and Ten Kingdoms	五代十国	wǔ dài shí guó	907 - 960
Northern Song Dynasty	北宋	běi sòng	960 - 1127
Southern Song Dynasty	南宋	nán sòng	1127 - 1279
Liao Dynasty	辽	liáo	916 - 1125
Jin Dynasty	金	jīn	1115 - 1234
Yuan Dynasty	元	yuán	1271 - 1368
Ming Dynasty	明	míng	1368 - 1644
Qing Dynasty	清	qīng	1644 - 1912

After the Qin Dynasty, came the great Han Dynasty, which was founded in 206 B.C. Emperor Wu of Han restored Confucianism and made it the only state philosophy. He also set up universities, honoring and employing scholars in government. Of course, he was more famous for his military feats. An important route to west, the Silk Road, was established during his reign. The Silk Road starts from China, passes India, and winds across Central Asia to Baghdad, Alexandria and Rome. Despite its name, the Silk Road provided a vital trade route for many other commodities apart from silk, from gold and ivory to exotic animals and plants.

The Tang Dynasty existed from the 7th to 9th century. At that time, China was the most secure and civilized country in the world. The empire had reached its largest size to date. The emperors accepted an open diplomacy policy, promoting communication with foreign countries and civilizations. In addition, the Silk Road was most prosperous during the Tang Dynasty. This prosperity and openness led to a flourishing culture, art, architecture, sculpture and literature all experienced a golden age during this time.

Today, China remains largely as mysterious and unknown as it was in the 19th Century, when gunboat diplomacy by foreign superpowers forced the last tottering dynasty to open up to foreign trade and exploration. Condemned to pay enormous indemnities and humiliated in every possible way by its European neighbors, the Chinese people rose in rebellion in the year 1911. Another turning point of Chinese history came on October 1st, 1949, when the People's Republic of China was founded, unveiling a new era of this ancient nation.

History and politics aside, China is a land of superlatives, encompassing the Yangtze River, the Silk Road, the bamboo forests of the giant panda and misty peaks immortalized in traditional ink paintings. China has thirty-eight UNESCO World Heritage Sites. Chinese food ranks among the world's great cuisines. From acrobatics to martial arts, calligraphy to Chinese opera, the vibrant, distinctive culture of this great land is everywhere to be seen.

014

Chinese Architecture

The basic distinguishing feature of Chinese architecture is rectangular units of space joined together as a whole. While temples in ancient Greece also employed rectangular spaces, the Chinese style combines rectangular shapes varying in size and position according to importance of a room with regards to the whole building. Each level and component is clearly distinguished, and as a result, traditional Chinese-style buildings have an imposing yet dynamic exterior.

The way units of space are combined in traditional Chinese architecture follows the principles of balance and symmetry. The main structure is the axis, and secondary structures are positioned as two wings on each side to form the main rooms and yard. Residences, official buildings, temples, and palaces all follow these same basic principles.

The Hall of Prayer for Good Harvest in the Temple of Heaven is one of the most amazing buildings in Chinese architecture history.

The distribution of interior space reflects Chinese social and ethical values. For instance, in traditional residential buildings, members of a family are assigned living quarters based on the family hierarchy. The master of the house occupies the main room, and the elder members of the master's family live in the compound to the rear. The younger members of the family live in the wings to the left and right - those with seniority on the left and the others on the right.

Yellow Crane Tower, located in Wuhan, is one of the Four Great Towers in China.

Another characteristic of traditional Chinese architecture is its use of wooden frames on the interior and exterior pillars, beams, and earthen walls surrounding the building on three sides. The main door and windows are in the front of the building. The Chinese have used wood as the main construction material for thousands of years. To the Chinese, wood represents life, and "life" is a vital component of Chinese culture. In order to preserve the wooden structure, lacquers were made in brilliant, bold colors, and became one of the key identifying features of traditional Chinese architecture.

Roofs usually slope down on both sides in a simple fashion. However, many traditional Chinese buildings have curved eaves. The characteristic curve of Chinese roofs is symbolic of the spirit of Chinese culture. While the building itself is relatively plain and straightforward, the peaked roof and upward-curving eaves introduce a sense of sophistication and artistry. This is analogous to the Chinese national character, which is by nature plain and straightforward, but still full of vitality.

The Hall of Supreme Harmony in the Palace Museum

Different colored murals found on a traditional Chinese building range from outlines of dragons and phoenixes, to depictions of myths, to paintings of landscapes, flowers and birds. These multicolored murals have both symbolic and aesthetic significance. One notable architectural development in southern China, particularly in Taiwan, is fine wood sculpture. Such sculptures coupled with murals give the structure an elegant and ornate effect.

As with many other elements of the Chinese culture, tradition has been mixed with modern technology. Although many traditional buildings still exist, almost all new buildings are built with Western-style architecture. All of China's large cities now have a wealth of modern skyscrapers.

The Origin of Chinese Characters

In contrast to Western words composed of phonetic letters, Chinese characters are made of several components to form a square shape, and can indicate pronunciation, meaning, or both. Chinese characters provide a convenient tool for imagery thinking.

With language, ancient humans began accumulating knowledge through which human culture arose. With characters, they recorded the language and communicated with each other, which distinguished human beings from animals. It is a character that drew a line between the primitive and civilized periods of human society.

There are various sayings in ancient Chinese documents concerning the origin of Chinese characters. The legendary story recorded in ancient Chinese books tells of Cang Jie, a history officer of the Yellow Emperor, who invented Chinese characters.

Historians in the past once tried to prove whether there was a person named Cang Jie in history, and if he did exist, when he lived, but they failed to draw a conclusion due to lack of irrefutable proof. Evidently

A picture shows how Chinese character developed from the top to the bottom

A portrait of Cang Jie

Ancient Chinese character - Jiaguwen, inscribed on tortoise shell

Jiaguwen inscribed on animal bones

the legend of Cang Jie cannot be accepted as the truth, for any script can only be a creation developed by people to meet the needs of social life over a long period of trial and error. Chinese characters are a huge and complicated system, and they could only have come into being after a long period of creation and development.

According to modern researchers, the ancestors of the Chinese people tied knots in rope to record events. Later, they adopted sharp weapons to inscribe signs, and developed the earliest form of Chinese characters. Archeologists have found inscribed signs on Neolithic pottery shards in Banpo Village in Shaanxi Province. These signs, dating back 6,000 years, were possibly the seeds of later Chinese characters.

Mathematics in Ancient China

Mathematics in China emerged independently by the 11th Century BC. The Chinese independently developed very large and negative numbers, decimals, a decimal system, a binary system, algebra, geometry, and trigonometry.

Simple mathematics inscribed on tortoise shells date back to the Shang Dynasty (1600 BC-1050 BC). One of the oldest surviving mathematical works is the *I Ching (Yi Jing)*, which included a sophisticated use of hexagrams.

Since early times, the Chinese had already fully developed a decimal system, understood basic arithmetic, algebra, equations, and negative numbers. Although the Chinese were more focused on arithmetic and advanced algebra for astronomical use, they were also the first to develop negative numbers, algebraic geometry and the usage of decimals.

Mathematics was one of the "Six Arts" that students were required to master during the Zhou Dynasty. Learning them all perfectly was required to be a gentleman, or in the Chinese sense, a "Renaissance Man". The Six Arts have their roots in the Confucian philosophy.

Chinese mathematics and the mathematics of the ancient Mediterranean world had developed more or less independently up to the time when the *The Nine Chapters on the Mathematical Art (Jiu Zhang Suan Shu)* reached its final form. It is often suggested that some

Zu Chongzi - one of the greatest mathematicians in China, who made great contribution to the computation of pi.

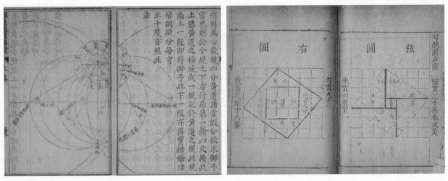

Chinese ancient mathematics draft   Pythagorean theorem draft

Chinese mathematical discoveries predate their Western counterparts. One example is the Pythagorean theorem. There is some controversy regarding this issue and the precise nature of this knowledge in early China. The Chinese were one of the most advanced in dealing with mathematical computations, and created enormous numbers. Elements of "Pythagorean" science have been found, for example, in one of the oldest Classical Chinese texts - King Wen sequence. This book was known for all of the mathematical information it contained. Knowledge of Pascal's triangle has also been shown to have existed in China centuries before Pascal.

017

The Abacus

The Abacus, also known as "counting frame", "calculating board" or "calculating table", is an ancient calculating device formerly used all over the world. Invented by the Chinese, the first record of the abacus was from a sketch of one in a book from the Yuan Dynasty (14th century). Its Chinese name is "Suan Pan" which means "calculating plate". Its inventor is unknown, but the abacus is often referred to as the "first computer" because it was used as a mathematic model for early electronic computers.

The abacus is typically constructed of various types of hardwoods and comes in varying sizes. The frame of the abacus has a series of vertical rods on which a number of wooden beads are allowed to slide freely. A horizontal beam separates the frame into two sections, known as the upper deck and the lower deck.

The standard abacus can be used to perform addition, subtraction, division and multiplication; the abacus can also be used to extract squareroots and cubic roots. It was originally a dust board, a board

A wooden abacus

Pupils are practicing abacus.

covered with dust or wax in which to trace figures, functioning as a writing pad in nowadays. Later, it became a board with grooves in which to slide counters back and forth. Finally, it became the familiar abacus, a wooden frame with beads on rods. In modern times, it has fallen out of use, being replaced by written arithmetic and, more recently, calculators. However, it is still used in many Asian countries.

The Ancient Chinese Economy

For over 4,000 years, China has been a nation of farmers. China's development of farming over the course of its history played a key role in supporting its growth. Throughout its history various methods have been developed or imported that enabled greater farming production and efficiency.

Agriculture:

China has placed an emphasis on agriculture and restraint on industry during its long feudal history. As a result, various methods developed that enabled greater production and efficiency. In addition, extensive irrigation systems were built to facilitate agriculture, such

Wheat was one of the most important commercial crops in ancient China.

as The Grand Canal and Dujiangyan Irritation System which have benefited people for thousands years. Governments in all the dynasties constantly implemented new and innovative land policies to promote the farming economy.

Commerce:

Both the rapid development of agriculture and the handicraft industry provided a wealth of domestic business and foreign trade. The main commodities included foodstuffs, salt, spirits, tea, medicine, textiles, gold or silver ware and some daily items. A large number of commercial sites sprang up. Meanwhile, due to the opening up of the Silk Road in the Han Dynasty (206 BC - 220 AD), vast numbers of foreign merchants and envoys came to trade in China. This also promoted the development of the marine trade. At that time, Tang ships could traverse the Indian Ocean and reach the Persian Gulf. Merchant ships traded frequently

Agriculture was the economic backbone in ancient China.

between China and countries in Asia and Africa. For this reason, it is considered that the Silk Road in its prime was central to the global economic system, as Chinese silks, rugs, spices, herbs, and ceramics made it to Europe from East Asia, sparking interest of Europeans in this far off exotic land.

Jiaozi

Jiaozi: the earliest paper currency in the world

China was the first country in the world to use paper currency, called Jiaozi. The history of Jiaozi dates back to the Northern Song Dynasty (960 - 1127). With the high circulation of the currency, the local government of Chengdu established the earliest administrative and savings bank known as the Office of Jiaozi. Paper money proved popular in the later dynasties like the Yuan, Ming, and Qing, but it never replaced the metal coins in circulation.

Jinshang: creating China's commercial culture

The term Jinshang is a tribute given to merchants from Shanxi Province for their achievements in building China's commercial culture. Although they lived in closed residences, their sense of business possibility was not restricted. It was the Shanxi merchants who first established the Piaohao (early banks) in China.

It was during the Ming and the Qing dynasties that the Jinshang reached their period of great prosperity. Their footsteps not only covered China but also reached Japan, Southeast Asia, Arabia, and Europe. Their business interests ranged from salt, iron, cotton, silk, and tea to various financial endeavors, including pawnshops, private banks, and account bureaus.

019

Early Chinese Banks

Ever since the 5th Century, China has had many different types of financial institutions that deal with mortgage, loans, credit and money exchange. Three main kinds of banking institution competed in ancient China's financial market.

Dangpu

Dangpu lived on small mortgage lending. Originating in the 5th Century and driven by mortgages, Dangpu were set up by politicians, aristocrats, wealthy businessmen and even temple monks who hoped to profit from interest rates and make money. Dangpu, both private and governmental, thrived for nearly all of China's long history. However, they mostly targeted poor lower-class people, providing small loans and some money exchange for gold, silver and copper. Strict guidelines were

Rishengchang was the first Piaohao opened in China, and also an originator of Chinese modern banks.

A statue of Zhanggui - the owner of Dangpu

enforced to manage Dangpu to protect the poor. For example, it was forbidden for Dangpu to quit business during a famine to protect the poor who had urgent need for a mortgage.

Piaohao

As the society progressed, heavy metal money became quite inconvenient for carrying and long distance transportation, thus the earliest paper money appeared in 1024. The first Piaohao originated in Pingyao, Shanxi Province. To deal with the transfer of large amounts of cash from one branch to another, the company introduced drafts, cashable in the company's many branches around China. Although this new method was originally designed for business transactions within the

Xiyuecheng Company, it became so popular that in 1823 the owner gave up the dye business altogether and reorganized the company as a special remittance firm, Rishengchang Piaohao.

Qianzhuang

Independent of the nationwide network of Piaohao there were a large number of small native banks, generally called Qianzhuang. These institutions first appeared in the Yangtze Delta region, in Shanghai, Ningbo, and Shaoxing. The first Qianzhuang can be traced to at least the mid-eighteenth century. In 1776, several of these banks in Shanghai organized themselves into a guild under the name of Qianye Gongsuo. In contrast to Piaohao, most Qianzhuang were local and functioned as commercial banks by conducting local money exchange, issuing cash notes, exchanging bills and notes, and providing discounts for the local business community.

Qianzhuang maintained close relationships with Chinese merchants, and grew with the expansion of China foreign trade. When Western banks first entered China, they issued "chop loans" to the Qianzhuang, who would then lend this money to Chinese merchants who used it to purchase goods from foreign firms. It is estimated that there were around 10,000 Qianzhuang in China in the early 1890s.

Chinese Ancient Coinage

Chinese coinage is one of the oldest currencies in the world, with more than 3,000 years of history. There have been many types of coins throughout Chinese history, such as Bei Bi (cowry shells), Dao Bi (knives), Bu Bi (spades), Yi Bi Qian (ant nose money), Ban Liang, Jiao Zi, Tong Bi (bronze coin), Yin Bi (silver coin) and so on. Today, we can see how the development of the Chinese coinage reflects the rising and falling fortunes of successive dynasties in Chinese history.

With the opening of markets between farmers, artisans, and merchants, cowry shells became the earliest currency in China. Inscriptions and archaeological evidence show that cowry shells were regarded as important objects of value in the Shang Dynasty. Cowry shells entered the stage of history in the Spring and Autumn period. During this time, there were many separate societies and cultures across China, so the types of coin were highly diversified, from Dao Bi, Bu Bi to Yi Bi Qian.

Ban Liang - a circular coin with square hole in the middle - was the first national currency of China. It is associated with the first Chinese Emperor, Qin Shi Huang Di, who united China in 221 BC. He abolished the Dao Bi, Bu Bi, Yi Bi Qian and other coins used in different

Kai Yuan Tong Bao, Tang Dynasty (618-907)

Xian Feng Yuan Bao, Qing
Dynasty (1644-1912)

regions and spread Ban Liang all over China. Since then, the shape of the Ban Liang has been a symbol of ancient Chinese coins.

With the changing of dynasties, Chinese ancient coinage changed names many times, from Yuan Bao, to Tong Bao, to Sheng Bao and so on, and was cast in various materials including gold, silver, bronze, iron and lead, though its circular shape with a square hole remained unchanged. Coin casting was well developed in the Song Dynasty. The bronze coin was especially notable, as it became the main basis of the Song monetary system.

China's first paper currency, named Jiao Zi, emerged in the Northern Song Dynasty. In the Ming Dynasty, silver and paper money replaced bronze coins as the main currency used in large transactions, and bronze coins were used only for small transactions. Silver was the official currency of China until the Qing Dynasty collapsed.

021

Chinese Lunar Calendar

The Chinese Lunar Calendar is the longest chronological record in history, dating from 2600 B.C., when Emperor Huang introduced the first cycle of the zodiac calendar. Like the Western calendar, the Chinese Lunar Calendar is a yearly calendar. It is based on a unique combination of astronomy and geography established through observation and exploration. It is also referred to as the Agriculture calendar, Yin calendar, Xia calendar or the old Chinese calendar.

All calendars are a system to measure the passage of time, from short durations of minutes and hours, to intervals of time measured in days, months, years and centuries. These are based on the astronomical observations of the movement of the sun, moon and stars.

Days are measured by the duration of time of one self-rotation of the earth. Months are measured by the duration of time it takes the moon to rotate around the earth. Years are measured by the duration of time it takes for the earth to rotate around the sun.

The concept of a "week" is less important in the Chinese calendar than in the Western calendar. The ancient Chinese had a ten-day week. Each month, the moon changes from "New Moon" to "Full Moon" and back. As a result, a month is simply called "a moon" in the Chinese language. A normal year has twelve lunar months. In order to add up to 365.24 days, an extra month is added during the leap year.

Chinese lunar calendar was established by the movement of the moon.

A Gregorian-Chinese calendar

The Chinese calendar has been in continuous use for centuries. It predates the International calendar (based on the Gregorian calendar) in use at the present, which goes back only some 430 years. The ancient Chinese invented the lunar calendar as a result of a long-term observation of astronomy, with the goal of maximizing the time used for farming, as China historically was an agriculturally based country.

In most of East Asia today, the Gregorian calendar is used for day-to-day activities, but the Chinese calendar is still used for marking traditional East Asian holidays. It is not unusual to find that many Chinese festivals are related to the moon, especially the first (New Moon) and fifteenth day (Full Moon) of the lunar month. Chinese New Year falls on the first day of the first lunar month, while Moon Cake Festival falls on the fifteenth day of the eighth lunar month.

The Chinese calendar is still used for choosing the most auspicious date weddings or the opening of a new building. Because each month follows one cycle of the moon, it is also used to determine the phases of the moon.

24 Solar Terms

As Chinese calendar is a lunisolar calendar that is based on both the movement of the sun and moon. Because of this, it couldn't fully reflect the operation of the sun. However, ancient Chinese people survived on agriculture, which required detailed knowledge of seasonal changes that are indicated by solar changes. So the "24 solar terms" came into being as a supplement in traditional calendar, mainly for guiding farming.

During the course of the year, the day when the shadow of a sundial is the shortest is the summer solstice; the day when the shadow is the longest is the winter solstice; the day when the shadow is of medium length is either the vernal equinox or the autumnal equinox. These solar terms were documented in the ancient book of the Spring and Autumn Period, The Classic of History.

The 24 solar terms are special terms created by ancient working people of China to reflect the changes of weather, climate and natural phenomena. The terms are closely related to agricultural production and every aspect of daily life, including clothing, food, housing and transportation.

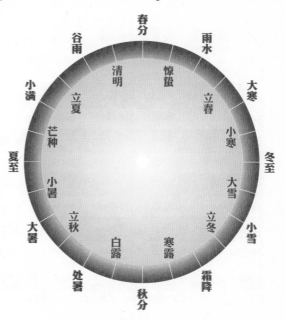

The position of 24 solar terms on the Chinese zodiac

Translation	Chinese name	Date	Remark
Start of Spring	立春	4-Feb	the beginning of spring
Rain Water	雨水	19-Feb	the gradual increase of rainfalls.
Awakening of Insects	惊蛰	6-Mar	a relatively fast temperature rise and possible spring thunders
Vernal Equinox	春分	21-Mar	the equal length of day and night.
Clear and Bright	清明	5-Apr	clear skies, fresh air, warm weather and lush plants
Grain Rain	谷雨	20-Apr	the increase of rainfalls, which is good for grain crops.
Start of Summer	立夏	6-May	the beginning of summer
Grain Full	小满	21-May	the seeds of summer crops are getting plump but not ripe yet
Grain in Ear	芒种	6-Jun	the ripening of wheat crops and the beginning of a busy farming season
Summer Solstice	夏至	21-Jun	the extreme of summer in astronomical terms
Minor Heat	小暑	7-Jul	the hottest days are yet to come.
Major Heat	大暑	23-Jul	the hottest time of the year
Start of Autumn	立秋	8-Aug	beginning of autumn
Limit of Heat	处暑	23-Aug	summer is coming to an end.
White Dew	白露	8-Sep	the temperature begins to fall, the weather is getting cold and there are dewdrops on grass and trees in the morning
Autumnal Equinox	秋分	23-Sep	the equal length of day and night
Cold Dew	寒露	8-Oct	lower temperature, dew in the air and cold feeling.
Frost Descent	霜降	23-Oct	the appearance of frost
Start of Winter	立冬	7-Nov	the beginning of winter
Minor Snow	小雪	22-Nov	the beginning of light snowfalls.
Major Snow	大雪	7-Dec	the beginning of heavy snowfalls
Winter Solstice	冬至	22-Dec	the extreme of winter in astronomical terms.
Minor cold	小寒	6-Jan	the weather is getting colder, but the coldest days are yet to come
Major cold	大寒	20-Jan	the coldest time of the year

A table shows the dates of 24 solar terms

023

Chinese Ancient Clocks

More than 2,200 years ago, Chinese people started to use the sun to determine the time. In the Qin (221-207 BC) and Han (206 BC-AD 220) dynasties, the sundial had become popular. The sundial, which measures the time of day by the direction of shadows cast by the sun, is a round plate with a needle embedded in the center. Under the sun, the shadow of the needle moves slowly on the surface of the sundial to indicate time. A well-designed sundial can measure local solar time with reasonable accuracy, and sundials continued to be used to monitor the performance of clocks until the modern era.

When it was cloudy or at night, the sundial does not function, so what could people use to measure time? The clepsydra, also known as water thief or water clock, was a timekeeping device used even earlier than sundials. The earliest outflow clepsydra was found in the Zhou Dynasty (1122-256 BC). But it was replaced with the inflow clepsydra due to low accuracy. The inflow clepsydra with an indicator rod on a float had been known in China since the beginning of the Han Dynasty in 202 BC. The earliest inflow clepsydra existed was found in Yuan Dynasty (1271-1368). It consisted of a four-level copper pot stand holding

An ancient sundial

water, with small holes at the bottom for water to drip through. People could tell the time through the rod scale above the water. The inflow clepsydra improved accuracy, and the more levels the clepsydra has, the more accurate it is to measure time.

As the method of measuring time through clepsydra still had limitations, a mechanism was adopted in clepsydra to comply with astronomical purposes. The water clock was probably the oldest time-measuring instrument.

Chinese people also used the armillary sphere in aiding calendar calculations and observations of celestial movements. The world's first water-powered celestial globe was created by Zhang Heng in 125, who is the first person known to have applied hydraulic motive power to rotate an armillary sphere. Though the water-powered armillary sphere created by Zhang Heng was not just a clock, due to its astronomical functions. In Song Dynasty, Su Song (1020-1101) invented the water-driven astronomical clock tower, which employed the use of an early escapement mechanism. Su's armillary sphere was the first to be provided

The bronze clepsydra found in Yuan Dynasty (1271-1368)

A scale model of Su Song's Astronomical Clock Tower

A model of water-powered armillary sphere created by Zhang Heng

with a mechanical clock drive, and also featured the oldest known endless power-transmitting chain drive. However, the clock itself was destroyed in a war. There's a common belief that advanced mechanical clockworks were brought from Europe. Although not as prominent as in the Song period, contemporary Chinese texts of the Ming Dynasty (1368-1644) describe a relatively unbroken history of designs of mechanical clocks in China from the 13th to the 16th centuries.

Heavenly Stems and Earthly Branches

The Chinese sexagenary cycle is a cyclic numeral system of 60 combinations of the two basic cycles, the 10 Heavenly Stems (Tian Gan) and the 12 Earthly Branches (Di Zhi). These two sets of terms were used to name the years of the civil calendar. Combining these series forms a greater cycle of 60 terms, as the least common multiple of 10 and 12 is 60. The first term is formed by adding the first stem to the first branch, then the second stem to the second branch, and so on. This was how the tradition of celebrating the 60th birthday began.

The eight trigrams of Bagua.

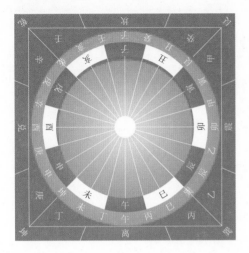

A map shows the Chinese Sexagenary cirlcle

The five nature of objects:metal, wood, water, fire and earth

This traditional Chinese system is used as a means of numbering days and years, not only in China but also in other East Asian countries. The Sexagenary system is also important in Chinese astrology and Chinese fortune telling. This counting system employing things of nature and animals create many myths, and people today still consider the good and bad luck of certain days and years.

The cycle has been used in China since the second millennium BC, as a means of naming days. This use of the cycle for days was attested for throughout the Zhou Dynasty. For instance, most entries in the Spring and Autumn Annals use this system. Its use for recording years is more recent. It became widespread in the Western Han Dynasty (202 BC - AD 8), and might have begun in the late Warring States period. The first day of a new year in the sexagenary cycle should be the Lichun. The year 1984 began the present cycle, and 2044 will begin another.

025

Ancient Education and the Imperial Examination System

Thousands years ago when Chinese characters were invented, informal schools began to form to teach people how to read and write. In the Xia Dynasty, some places' solely purpose was to teach, and they were the first schools in ancient Chinese history.

In the beginning all schools were public schools. Nobles and the common people went to different public schools. In the Spring and Autumn Period, private schools appeared and distinguished scholars spread their philosophies through their private schools. In the succeeding years, private schools continued to exist, although public schools were more mainstream.

In the Han Dynasty, the central government created an education system where students mainly studied the classical Confucian books. Top students were given official titles directly after examinations. At this time examinations were merely done through observation. Local officials recommended students they considered intelligent to their superior. Obviously, this method could easily lead to nepotism and corruption. There had to be a new way of selection.

The Imperial Examination System was invented in the Sui Dynasty. It dominated ancient Chinese education immediately after its creation. Originally people from lower classes had little chance to move to the upper classes as government officials. Once the Imperial Examination system was introduced, all males could take the tests and had opportunities to become government officials, regardless of parentage and age. This system influenced many other Asian countries including Korea and Japan. Today's education system is surely its successor.

Imperial Examination Compound

There were a total of three stages leading up to realizing the dream of becoming an official: the Provincial examination, the Metropolitan examination, and the Palace examination by the emperor. The Metropolitan examination was held in autumn. In the following spring the qualifying candidates would go to the capital for the Palace examination. To prevent the practice of favoritism, student names were covered and papers were reviewed by different examiners. This reduced the possibility of cheating greatly.

The system was refined gradually. In the Tang Dynasty the main subjects of the examinations were writing and the study of classical books, as well as mathematics, law, and calligraphy. Students who passed the highest imperial examination would have a promising future. In the Song Dynasty, the frequency of tests was limited to once every three

One of the Imperial Examination
Compounds, located in Confucius
Temple, Nanjing

years. With the coming of the Ming Dynasty, the Imperial Examination
System reached its period of full bloom. Great attention was given to the
administrative procedures and tests became more rigorous.

The system prevailed for more than 1,300 years and finally
declined in the Qing Dynasty. The system makes sense in ancient rural
societies where changes in all aspects of life are slow, but it doesn't fit
into the modern industrialized societies where changes are much faster.
The last imperial examination in China was held in 1904, and after that
it was abolished. All public schools now operate by modern standards
of education.

026

Six Arts in Ancient China

Ancient Confucianism put a large emphasis on education. Generally speaking, Confucian education stressed six subjects in school, called the "Six Arts". They are 礼Rites, 乐Music, 射Archery, 御Charioteering, 书Calligraphy, and 数Mathematics. Under the influence of Confucianism, students were required to learn and attain comprehensive knowledge of these subjects.

1. 礼 Rites

Rites include politics, morality, patriotism and customs of the society.

2. 乐 Music

Music includes music, dance, poetry, and so on.

A scene of music performing depicted in an ancient Chinese painting

3. 射 **Archery**

This subject can be seen as a preparation for ancient military activities.

4. 御 **Charioteering**

In addition to archery training, charioteering was also for military use and required students learn to drive a chariot.

5. 书 **Calligraphy**

书 literally means "book" and this subject includes reading, writing, drawing and calligraphy.

A portrait of ancient archery

6. 数 **Mathematics**

数 contains various subjects related to science and technology.

China's ancient "Six Arts" emphasized comprehensive development in all subject areas, and attempted to educate students to be well-rounded. At the same time, different arts were learned and practiced at different ages. For example, Rites, Music, Archery and Charioteering together are called "Big Arts". These were compulsory subjects for aristocracy who wanted to go into politics. Studying the Big Arts required great depth, and perseverance to reach the highest levels. "Small Arts", including Calligraphy and Mathematics, were learned for daily use, and were compulsory in primary school. At that time, the common people's children only received "Small Arts" education. Only the aristocracy could complete both "Big Arts" and "Small Arts" training. Although the Six Arts functioned to enforce social hierarchy, it still served to advance education for the Chinese people.

Ancient Confucianism shapes the educational philosophy in China even today. Regardless of the advantages and limitations the Six Arts has, it indeed gave us a long-lasting standard that in order to succeed, one needs comprehensive knowledge, unwavering morality and a wide range of skills.

027

The Ancient Chinese Way to Address Teachers

China has a long history of giving teachers great respect. Since ancient times, education was given great importance. Ordinary people wanted their children to get a good education, so that they would one day bring honor to the family. As early as 3,000 years ago, there were multitudes of different official and private schools all over the country. There is an old Chinese saying 三人行，必有我师, which literally means "among any three people walking, I will definitely find something to learn." In the ancient times, there were many ways to address a teacher. Here are several interesting ways to address teachers:

1. 先生(xiān sheng)
先 means before. According to tradition, students should respect and honor their teachers in all cases, thus this word connotes the idea that a student will put their teacher first before all else. It was frequently used in the late 19th and 20th Centuries to address teacher respectfully. Even today, it's usually used among people who learn martial arts, and traditional arts like Peking opera and Quyi.

2. 师父 (shī fu)
The word 师父(shīfu) is the way for students to bestow honor upon teachers of crafts. It is interesting that the word has a 父, which means father, implying how important teachers are in a student's life.

3. 祭酒 (jì jiǔ)
This term used to refer to an official government position of education, and later came to mean teacher. The word literally means

An ancient private school

sacrifice with wine. Ancient people regarded sacrificial activities as one of the most important things in their lives, so equating a teacher with the master of sacrificial ceremonies conveyed great respect.

028

Confucius

Confucius is undoubtedly the greatest single influence over the Chinese character. Aside from being a great educator and thinker, he was first of all a noble moralist. He pursued truth, kindness and perfection throughout his life and his successes and failures were largely due to his character, which had an everlasting impact on Chinese intellect.

Confucius was born in 551 B.C. in the State of Lu, which is known today as Qufu in Shandong province. In Chinese, his name was Kong Qiu. Kong was the family name while Qiu was his given name. Sadly, his father died when Confucius was very young, but despite a hard life, he dedicated himself to his studies at the age of 15.

Patriotism drove the young Confucius, and he set his sights on an official career as a means of putting his political ideals into effect. He had gained some fame by the time he was 30, but it was not until he was 51 that his official life really assumed great importance. But his success was short-lived; after only four years he was forced to resign when he found it impossible to agree with the authorities. Such was the opposition to his ideas that he was forced to leave his country and travel around the various states that now make up China. During the following 14 years, he was in danger on many occasions and even risked his life. At the

A portait of Confucius

age of 68 he was welcomed back to Lu, but he was set up as a respected gentleman without any authority. He died of illness at the age of 73, a brilliant star falling into silence. His students treated him as father and wore willow sprigs for three years in mourning. Zigong, one of his famous disciples, set up a residence near his tomb and stayed there for six years to mourn his beloved teacher. Confucius could never have dreamed that his lonely tomb would later develop into the large Cemetery of Confucius, and that his ideological system would become the norm for Chinese society for thousands of years.

Compared to his frustrated political career, Confucius' career as a teacher and philosopher was brilliant and full of achievements.

Much of his approach to education was before its time, as he promoted the ideas "to educate all despite their social status" and "to teach according to the students' characteristics." The first of these broke with tradition, as only the aristocracy had the privilege of education at that time.

Confucius also proposed a complete set of principles concerning studying. He said, "Studying without thinking leads to confusion; thinking without studying leads to laziness."

Confucius' Temple

A statue of Confucius in front of the Confucius' Temple

Imparting knowledge was only part of his teaching; he was also a living example of the concepts he promoted, and this had a deep and lasting influence upon his disciples. Confucius' private life was a model of his doctrines. *The analects of Confucius* provides a vivid record of his teachings, although he wrote nothing personally, his words were collected and recorded for posterity by his disciples. The accumulated words of wisdom have come down to us as analects, one of the most important of all the Chinese classics.

029

The Analects

*T*he Analects (Lun Yu), also known as the *Analects of Confucius*, are a record of the words and deeds of the iconic Chinese thinker and philosopher Confucius and his disciples, as well as a record of the discussions they held.

Written from the Spring and Autumn Period through the Warring States Period, *The Analects* is the representative work of Confucianism and continues to have a tremendous influence on China today. Since Confucius' time, *The Analects* has heavily influenced the philosophy and moral values of China and other East Asian countries. Together with the other three volumes of *The Four Books*, it taught the basic Confucian values including propriety, righteousness, loyalty and filial piety, all stemming from the central element of Confucianism - humanity.

Confucius 3,000 disciples reciting "The Analects of Confucius" in Beijing Olympic Games opening ceremony

A painting depicting one of Confucius' words and deeds

For almost 2,000 years, *The Analects* was also the foundation of study for all Chinese scholars, a man was not considered morally upright or enlightened if he did not study Confucius' works. The imperial examination (Ke Ju), used in ancient Chinese society to select government officials also strongly emphasized Confucian studies and expected the candidates to quote and apply the thoughts and words of Confucius in their essays.

The Analects has also been translated into many languages, most notably into English and portions into Latin by Western Christian missionaries in the late 16th Century. It has been said that the book may well have been the first in human history to describe the life of an individual, historic personage. Confucius' conversations were the oldest complete intellectual and spiritual portrait of a man. Many scholars say that everything it contains and indeed everything it lacks is important.

China Earliest Soccer - Cuju

Cuju is an ancient game with similarities to modern soccer. It originated in China, and was also played in Korea, Japan and some other Asian countries. Some people argue that this primitive version of soccer existed in China centuries ago, and was later modified by English scholars in the mid-18th century to become modern soccer. But, regardless of whether these arguments are true, Cuju was a charming and unique ancient Chinese game.

The game of Cuju first emerged during the Warring States Period (476-221 BC). Cuju was both used as fitness training for soldiers, and as entertainment in wealthy cities. During the Han Dynasty (206 BC-AD 220), the popularity of Cuju spread from the army to the royal courts and upper classes. It is said that the emperor Wu of Han enjoyed the sport very much. The game was improved during the Tang Dynasty (618-907). At that time, Chang'an (the capital of Tang) was filled with Cuju soccer fields in the backyards of large mansions, and some were even established on the grounds of the palaces. In Song Dynasty (960-1279), Cuju flourished due to social and economic development, extending its popularity to the lower classes of society. At that time, professional Cuju players were quite popular, and the sport began to take on a commercial edge.

There are two ways to play Cuju. The first was commonly performed at court feasts celebrating the emperor's birthday or during diplomatic events. This competitive match between two teams consisted of 12 to 16 players on each side.

An ancient bronze craft depicts several people playing Cuju

An ancient painting describing how to play Cuju in Song Dynasty

The other form was the dominant Cuju style during the Song Dynasty, and it attached much more importance to developing personal skills, rather than scoring goals. However, Cuju began to decline during the Ming Dynasty (1368-1644), and due to neglect, the 2,000-year-old sport slowly faded away.

031

Chinese Antique Pillows

Chinese antique pillows are often hard boxes made from stone, wood, metal, or porcelain instead of stuffed fabric. The shape and contents of pillows have varied over time.

Shi Zhen (stone pillow), usually made from jade, were believed to translate the energy from the stone to the human brain. Derived in the Ming dynasty, this piece of material was trusted to cure headaches or depressions, or simply to better the intelligence of those who use it. It was more common in the royal and noble families because it was expensive and rare.

Mu Zhen (wood pillow) played an important role in ancient China. The shape of the wood pillow varied a lot, though it was made from precious woods like rosewood and boxwood. The boxwood pillow was often mentioned in ancient poems due to its rarity.

Among all Chinese antique pillows, Ci Zhen (porcelain pillow) was most widely used. It came into being with the development of porcelain-making crafts, and first appeared in the Sui Dynasty (581-618) and flourished in the Tang Dynasty. Porcelain pillows reached their climax in the Song Dynasty, featuring great variety and elegant modeling, including the geometrical shapes, animals, architectures, human figures and other shapes. It also had colorful decorative patterns including animals, plants, mountains and rivers and

Mu Zhen (wood pillow)

Tong Zhen (Bronze pillow)

Ci Zhen (Porcelain pillow)

A baby-shaped Ci Zhen (Porcelain pillow)

characters. The modeling and decorative patterns on the pillows directly or indirectly reflect the culture, customs, fashions, and pursuits of the social life at that time.

Most Chinese antique pillows were hard pillows, the ancient Chinese, however, thought that soft pillows robbed the body of vitality. However, modern Chinese people prefer soft pillows, often filled with natural stuffing like chaff, cotton, reedy flower and feather. Some are even filled with herbal remedies to cure disease and inspire sweet dreams.

032

Chinese Ethnic Groups

Similar to America, China is a tapestry of different nationalities and 56 distinct ethnic groups. Among them, Han people account for 1.2 billion people - 91 percent of the population. The other 55 ethnic groups span across approximately 100 million people, who account for 9 percent of China's population. Outside of Mandarin Chinese, 53 of these ethnic groups use spoken languages of their own and 23 ethnic groups have their own written languages.

Han people can be found in almost every part of China. However, they mainly live in the middle and lower reaches of the Yellow River, Yangtze River and the Pearl River, and in the Northeast Plain Region. They form the largest ethnic group within China and are the largest ethnic community in the world.

The Zang people celebrating their most important festival

Wax dyeing by the Miao people in Yunnan province

The Han people have their own spoken and written language, known as the Chinese language(汉语Hanyu), which is commonly used nowadays throughout China as the official national language. Hanyu has a history of 4,000 years, originating from pictographs. For most of their history, the Han have had an agricultural society, which was highly advanced, especially in irrigation and intensive farming. There was also a high level of early artistic production, such as bronze wares, silk, porcelain, architecture and painting. The Han culture belongs to the oldest civilization in the world, boasting outstanding achievements in fields including politics, military affairs, philosophy, literature, history, art and natural science, in addition to many others.

Although minority ethnic groups account for about 9 percent of the population, they are distributed over about 50 percent of Chinese territory, concentrated mostly in the border regions. Most of the minority ethnic groups live in the vast areas of the West, Southwest and Northwest. The largest minority group is the Zhuang people of southwestern China, who number 12 million.

Because equality, unity and common prosperity are the government's fundamental objectives in handling relations with minority ethnic groups, many minority groups live in compact communities and establish self-government to direct their own affairs.

Girls from the Yi group

An old Uigur carpenter

Each of the minority ethnic groups has a distinctive and rich character. For example, the Miao people are very skilled at handicrafts, such as embroidering, weaving, paper-cutting and jewelry casting. Miao embroidery and silver jewelry are delicate and beautiful. Their hats, collars, cuffs, skirts and even baby carriers, are embroidered with extremely colorful, complicated and cleanly sewn designs. Girls of around seven will learn embroidering from mothers and sisters, and by the time they become teenagers, they are masters of their craft. Clothes of the Miao ethnic minority are diverse and regionally specific. Men wear short coats and trousers, while women adorn themselves with dainty and dazzling skirts and jewels. Inspired by the natural world, their skirts are embroidered with intricate patterns of flowers and wildlife. These beautiful, pleated skirts can have as many as forty intricate layers!

033

Traditional Chinese Ways to Celebrate Birthdays

For thousands of years, the way that Chinese people reckoned age differed from the Western age reckoning system. The traditional way of counting a person's age in China is counted starting from conception, rather than from physical birth. Newborns start at one year old, and each passing of a Lunar Calendar's New Year, rather than the birthday, adds one year to the person's age. Such being the case, Chinese people usually are one or two years older than in the Western version.

Though most Chinese people reckon age and celebrate their birthdays in Western styles, some elders and conservative families still celebrate big birthdays in traditional ways. Big birthdays comes every 10 years, such as 30, 40, 50, 60 and 70, according to Chinese tradition, celebrations are only held for elders above 40 to show respect.

Confucius said, "At thirty, I stood firm. At forty, I had no doubts. At fifty, I know the decrees of Heaven. At sixty, my ear was an obedient organ for the reception of truth. At seventy, I could follow what my heart desired, without transgressing what was right." Important birthdays have been granted special meanings to Chinese people for thousands of years.

Except big family parties, special birthday foods are served during birthday celebrations for good wishes, Chang Shou Mian (longevity noodles) is the most remarkable one. The Chinese

Peach-shaped longevity buns

Chang Shou Mian (Longevity noodles)

character Chang (long) is also added as a prefix to represent "long life" (Chang Shou), while the character Mian (noodle) has another meaning of face in Chinese. In addition to noodles representing endless life, eating Chang Shou Mian implies that one has a long-life face. Besides Chang Shou Mian, children eat boiled eggs on birthdays and peach-shaped longevity buns are especially served at the birthday celebrations for elders.

Spring Festival

The Spring Festival is the most important festival for the Chinese people and is when all family members get together, similar to Christmas or Thanksgiving in the West. All people living far away from home return to their hometowns, making the weeks before and after Spring Festival the busiest time of the year for transportation systems. Airports, railway stations and long-distance bus stations are crowded to bursting with home returnees.

The Spring Festival falls on the first day of the first lunar month, often one month later than the first month of the Gregorian calendar. It originated in the Shang Dynasty (1600 B.C. - 1100 B.C.) from the people's sacrifice to gods and ancestors during the transition from the old year to the new year.

Spring Couplets and faux firecrackers

Spring Festival is a busy time for storeowners, as everybody goes out to purchase necessities for the New Year. Must-haves include cooking oil, rice, flour, chicken, duck, fish and meat, fruit, candies and all kinds of nuts. What's more, various decorations, new clothes and shoes for the children and gifts for the elderly, friends and relatives are all on the must-buy list.

Jiaozi

Before the New Year comes, people thoroughly clean the indoors and outdoors of their homes as well as their clothes, bedclothes and all their utensils. Then people begin decorating their homes, adding to the atmosphere of festivity. All the door panels are pasted with Spring Festival couplets, sayings written in Chinese calligraphy on red paper. The content varies from homeowners' wishes for a bright future, to wishing all good luck in the New Year. Aside from couplets, pictures of the god of doors and wealth will be posted on front doors to ward off evil spirits and welcome peace and abundance.

People attach great importance to New Year's Eve. At that time, all family members eat dinner together. The meal is more luxurious than usual. Dishes such as chicken, fish and tofu cannot be excluded, for in Chinese, their pronunciations, respectively "ji", "yu" and "doufu", mean auspiciousness, abundance and richness. After the dinner, the whole family will sit together, chatting and watching TV. In recent years, the Spring Festival Communist Party broadcast on China Central Television Station (CCTV) has become essential New Year's entertainment for the Chinese both at home and abroad. According to custom, each family will stay up until midnight to ring in the New Year.

Upon waking up on New Year's Day, everybody dresses up. First they extend greetings to their parents. Then each child will get money as a New Year gift, wrapped up in a red envelop. People in northern China will eat jiaozi, or dumplings, for breakfast, as they think "jiaozi" in sound means "bidding farewell to the old and ushering in the new." In addition, the shape of the dumplings is like the gold ingots of ancient China, so people eat them and wish for money and treasure.

Southern Chinese eat niangao, a New Year's cake made of glutinous rice flour, because niangao sounds like "higher and higher, one year after another." The first five days after the Spring Festival are a good time for relatives, friends, classmates and colleagues to exchange greetings, gifts and chat leisurely.

Lighting fireworks was once the most typical custom on Spring Festival. People thought the loud, cracking noise could help drive away evil spirits. However, setting off fireworks has been completely or partially forbidden in big cities since the government took security, noise and pollution into consideration. As a consolation, some buy tapes with firecracker sounds to listen to, some break little balloons to make a cracking sound, while others buy faux firecrackers to hang in their living room.

The lively atmosphere not only fills every household, but permeates the streets and lanes. A series of activities such as lion dancing, dragon lantern dancing, lantern festivals and temple fairs are held for days around Spring Festival. The Spring Festival comes to an end when the Lantern Festival is finished.

035

Mid-Autumn Festival

The Mid-Autumn Festival falls on the 15th day of the eighth lunar month. In ancient China, emperors followed the rite of offering sacrifices to the sun in spring and to the moon in autumn. Historical books as early as the Zhou Dynasty reference "Mid-Autumn". Later, aristocrats and literary figures helped expand the ceremony to common people. They enjoyed the full, bright moon on that day, worshipping it and expressing their thoughts and feelings under it. By the Tang Dynasty, the Mid-Autumn Festival had become fixed, and in the Song Dynasty (960 - 1279) it became even more important to the culture. In the Ming (1368-1644) and Qing (1644-1911) dynasties, it grew to be a major festival of China.

A traditional image of Chang E and her husband

Folklore about the origin of the festival tells an unusual story. In remote antiquity, there were ten suns rising in the sky, which scorched all the crops and drove people into dire poverty. A hero, named Hou Yi, using the full extent of his superhuman power, drew his extraordinary bow and shot down the nine superfluous suns one after another. He was respected and loved by the people, and many people with high ideals and integrity came to learn martial arts from him. Among them was an unsavory person named Peng Meng.

Moon cakes

Hou Yi had a beautiful and kindhearted wife named Chang E (pronounced Chang-Uh). One day on his way to the Kunlun Mountain to call on friends, he came upon the Empress of Heaven, Wangmu, who was passing by. Empress Wangmu presented to him an elixir that upon drinking, would cause one would ascend immediately to heaven and become a celestial being. Hou Yi, however, hated to part with his wife, so he gave the elixir to Chang E to treasure for the time being. Chang E hid the elixir in a treasure chest on her dressing table when, unexpectedly, it was seen by Peng Meng.

One day when Hou Yi led his disciples to go hunting, Peng Meng, sword in hand, rushed into the Chang E's inner chamber and to force her to hand over the elixir. Aware that she was unable to defeat Peng Meng, Chang E made a desperate decision. She turned to open her treasure box, took up the elixir and swallowed it in one gulp. As soon as she swallowed the elixir her body floated off the ground, dashed out the window and flew towards heaven. Meanwhile, Peng Meng escaped.

When Hou Yi returned home at dark, he found out from the maidservants what had happened. Overcome with grief, Hou Yi looked up into the night sky and called out the name of his beloved wife when, to his surprise, he found that the moon was especially clear and bight, and on it there was a swaying shadow that looked exactly like his wife. He tried his best to chase after the moon. But as he ran, the moon retreated; as he withdrew, the moon came back. He could never reach the moon.

Thinking of his wife day and night, Hou Yi had an incense table arranged in Chang E's beloved garden. He placed on the table Chang E's favorite sweetmeats and fresh fruits, and then held a memorial ceremony for Chang E, who was sentimentally still attached to him despite her distant home of the palace of the moon.

When people heard of the story that Chang E had turned into a celestial being, they arranged incense tables in the moonlight one after another and prayed to the kindhearted Chang E for good fortune and peace. From then on, the custom of worshiping the moon spread among the people.

People in different places follow various customs, but all show their love and longing for a better life. Today people enjoy the beauty of the full moon and eat moon cakes on that day.

The moon looks extremely round, big and bright on the 15th day of each lunar month. People selected August 15 to celebrate because it is a season when crops and fruits are ripe and the weather is pleasant. On the Mid-Autumn Festival, all family members or friends meet outside, set food out on tables and look up at the sky while talking about life. How splendid a moment it is!

Double Ninth Festival (Chongyang Jie)

Double Ninth Festival, called Chongyang Jie in Chinese, falls on the ninth day of the ninth month of the Chinese lunar calendar. It is a traditional Chinese holiday recorded on paper for more than 2,000 years.

According to the old philosophy of Yin and Yang, which are the two opposing principles in the world, nine is a Yang number which represents the masculine and positive power. So Double Ninth Day contains too much Yang, and is considered a dangerous date. In order to protect against the danger, it is customary for people to climb high hills, drink chrysanthemum wine, eat double-ninth cakes and wear the Zhuyu plant. Both chrysanthemum and the Zhuyu plant are believed to cleanse and cure illness.

Chrysanthemum

Double-ninth cakes (Chongyang Gao)

The festival is held in the golden season of autumn, at harvest time. The bright clear weather and the joy of bringing in the harvest make for a festive atmosphere. The Double Ninth Festival is usually perfect for outdoor activities. Many people go hiking and climbing in the country, enjoying Mother Nature's final burst of color before she puts on her dull winter cloak. Some will carry a sprig of dogwood.

The Double Ninth Festival is also a time when chrysanthemum flowers bloom. China boasts diversified species of chrysanthemum and people have loved them since ancient times. So enjoying the flourishing chrysanthemum is also a key activity during this festival. Many people will climb a mountain, appreciate the beautiful scenery of autumn and relax.

But what about those people who live in flat regions far from any mountain? This problem is solved by going for a picnic and eating cakes. The Chinese word for cake is Gao, a homonym of the Chinese word for high. Mountains are high, so eating cake can, by a stretch of the imagination, take the place of going for a climb. On that day, people always gather the whole family to spend the festival together, while those far from their homes will generally feel more homesick on that day.

In Chinese, the word "nine" is homophonous with the word for "long time", and accordingly this number has come to represent longevity. Thus, in 1966, the government designated Double Ninth Day as Senior Citizen's Day. Since then, Double Ninth Day has gradually lost its original purpose, becoming today a time of expressing gratitude to the elderly for their hard work and continuing the Chinese tradition of revering the old.

Tomb Sweeping Festival (Qingming Jie)

Tomb Sweeping Festival falls on the 15th day from the Spring Equinox. As one of the 24 solar terms, it is a sign the temperature will rise and rainfall will increase. "Qing Ming" literally means "Clear Brightness", hinting at its importance as a celebration of Spring. But the Qingming holiday is not only a seasonal point to guide farm work, it is more so a festival of commemoration. Tomb Sweeping Day celebrates the rebirth of nature, while marking the beginning of the planting season and other outdoor activities.

Tomb sweeping is regarded as the most important custom of the Qingming Festival. Following folk religion, the Chinese believed that the spirits of deceased ancestors looked after the family. Sacrifices of food and "spirit money" could keep them happy, and the family would prosper through good harvests and having more children. Cleaning the tomb and paying respects to the dead person with offerings are the two most important parts of remembering relatives. Cleaning the grave was just what it sounds like - removing weeds, making necessary repairs, and repainting the gravestone engravings. The dead person's favorite food and wine are taken to sacrifice to them, along with paper resembling money, called "spirit money". This

God's Lanterns

Incense to be lighted for sacrificing

A woman is praying by the tomb

was all burned in the hope that the deceased are not lacking food and money. The family would kowtow before the tablets set up for the dead.

Today, the custom has been extremely simplified in cities. Only flowers are presented to the dead relatives and revolutionary martyrs. No matter how respect is shown, good prayers for the deceased are expressed.

In contrast to the sadness of the tomb sweepers, people also enjoy the hopeful spirit of spring on this day. The Qingming Festival is a time when the sun shines brightly, the trees and grass become green and nature is again lively. Since ancient times, people have followed the custom of taking Spring outings, and at this time tourists are everywhere.

People love to fly kites during the Qingming Festival. Kite flying is actually not limited to the Qingming Festival. People fly kites not only during the day, but also at night. A string of little lanterns tied onto the kite or the kite string looks like shining stars, and therefore, are called "god's lanterns".

038

Chinese Valentine's Day (Qixi)

Valentine's Day isn't just for Westerners - the Chinese also have a holiday to celebrate love. Chinese Valentine's Day, also called "Qixi", falls on the evening of the seventh day of the seventh lunar month. This holiday commemorates a legendary pair of lovers, who were only allowed to see each other once a year on this day.

This holiday originates from a romantic tragedy of a cowherd and a weaver girl that took place on the "double seventh". The legend holds that one fairy girl (Zhinü) sneaked out of her heavenly home to the mortal world and took a low-paid weaver job in order to marry her humble lover Cowherd Boy (Niulang). They lived a happy life, the husband working on the farmland and the wife looking after kids and making clothes. It was the ideal model family from the perspective of traditional Chinese people. However, good things never last too long. What the fairy did had violated the rule of heaven, and thus deserved punishment by the queen of heaven, the fairy girl's mother. At last, the girl was forced to go back to heaven,

Niulang and Zhinü meet each once a year on the bridge

Magpie's bridge

and the boy was left on earth. The lovers were separated forever, and only allowed to meet once a year on the double seventh day. It is said at that night, the lover will reunion on the bridge which consists of the magpies.

Traditionally, people look up at the sky and find a bright star in the constellation Aquila and the star Vega, which are identified as Niulang and Zhinü. The two stars shine on opposite sides of the Milky Way. In old days, Qixi was more of a festival for girls. It was also known as the "Begging for Skills Festival" or "Daughters' Festival". Girls would conduct a ceremony to beg Zhinü for wisdom, dexterity and a happy marriage, offering the goddess fruit and pastries. In southern China, young women used to hold weaving and needlework competitions.

But nowadays, Qixi has been promoted as China's answer to St. Valentine's Day, though its original message - if there is one - has more to do with family values than love and passion. The story of the Cowherd Boy and the Weaver Girl is not about how to get married, but instead how to hold a family together. Even though the Niulang Zhinü legend colored with tragedy, it otherwise represents the ultimate devotion and pursuit of love. Recently many people have shown enthusiasm for Qixi, and are celebrating it anew, indicating the revival of Chinese traditions and customs.

Dragon Boat Festival (Duanwu Jie)

Together with Chinese New Year and Mid-Autumn Festival, Dragon Boat Festival forms one of the three major Chinese holidays. Also called Duanwu Jie in Chinese, it is celebrated on the fifth day of the fifth lunar month. There are many legends about this festival, of which the most widely known one is about the ancient patriotic poet Quyuan. Since summer

Zongzi

is a time when disease most easily spread, this festival has also been as an occasion for driving off evil spirits and disease.

For thousands of years, the festival has been marked by eating Zongzi and racing dragon boats. Other activities include carrying a fragrant bag (Xiang Bao), drinking Xionghuang Wine and hanging Calamus and Moxa in houses.

1. Zongzi

Zongzi, a pyramid-shaped glutinous rice dumpling wrapped in bamboo leaves that was said to commemorate the great patriot Quyuan. Quyuan was a loyal, patriotic and highly esteemed scholar and minister who was expelled from his own country because of scandal. After his country was conquered, he was in such despair that he committed suicide in the Miluo River. Nearby fishermen made Zongzi and threw them into the river, so that the fish would eat the rice rather than the hero poet.

Dragon boat racing

2. Dragon Boat Race

Dragon Boat Festival is highlighted by the dragon boat races, in which competing teams drive their boats forward rowing to the rhythm of pounding drums. The dragon-boat races symbolize the many attempts to rescue and recover Qu's body. A typical dragon boat ranges from 50-100 feet in length, with a width of about 5.5 feet, accommodating two paddlers seated side by side.

3. Carrying a Fragrant Bag (Xiang Bao)

It's believed that carrying a small fragrant bag around not only drives away evil spirits but also brings fortune and happiness to those who wear it. The small bags are hand-made by local craftsmen. They're made with red, yellow, green and blue silk, fine satin or cotton. Figures of animals, flowers and fruits are often embroidered onto the bags and inside are mixed Chinese herbal medicines.

4. Drinking Xionghuang Wine and Hanging Calamus and Moxa

Xionghuang Wine is a particular wine which is said to protect people from evil and disease. On this day, most of the families also hang calamus and moxa (oriental plants) on the front door. This is also to ward off evil.

040

Lantern Festival (Yuanxiao Jie)

Lantern Festival, also known as Yuanxiao Jie, takes place on the fifteenth day of the first lunar month. The 15th day is the first night to see a full moon. It also signals the end of spring festival celebrations. Numerous theories surround the festival's origins. It's possible that it was originally meant to honor Buddha.

Decorative Lanterns

The main attraction at the Lantern Festival is the lantern. Many lanterns are made to reflect historical Chinese themes, and depict scenes from stories and legends that express traditional values. They are also made to represent the 12 animals of the Chinese Zodiac and heroic figures. To highlight these glowing works of art, competitions are held. Today, the displaying of lanterns is still a big event on the 15th day of the first lunar month throughout China. People enjoy the brightly lit night.

Lantern Riddles

The Lantern Festival is further enriched by the customary lantern riddle parties. They are riddles that are stuck on the surface of some of the lanterns for people to guess. Historically, the subjects of the riddles were traditional songs, poems, stories or historical events. People very much enjoy the challenge of solving these riddles and lantern riddle parties are sometimes held at temples on the night of the Lantern Festival. These contents show that the lanterns not only provide aesthetic pleasure, but also serve to celebrate and express Chinese history and culture.

Yuanxiao (Glutinous Rice Balls)

Red lanterns

Yuanxiao

Besides entertainment and beautiful lanterns, another important part of the Lantern Festival is eating small dumpling balls made of glutinous rice flour. We call these balls Yuanxiao or Tangyuan. It is said that the custom of eating Yuanxiao originated during the Eastern Jin Dynasty in the 4th century, then became popular during the Tang and Song periods.

The fillings inside the dumplings or Yuanxiao are either sweet or salty. Sweet fillings are made of sugar, walnuts, sesame, rose petals, sweetened tangerine peel, bean paste, or jujube paste. A single ingredient or any combination can be used as the filling. The salty variety is filled with minced meat, vegetables or a mixture.

Decorative Lanterns

Yin-Yang and Directions

A ncient Chinese people were greatly interested in the relationships and patterns that occurred in nature. Instead of studying isolated things, they viewed the world as a harmonious and holistic entity. In their eyes, no single being or form could exist unless it was seen in relation to its surrounding environment. By simplifying these relationships, they tried to explain complicated phenomena in the universe.

"Yin-Yang" is one of the dominant concepts shared by different schools throughout the history of Chinese philosophy. The original concept of Yin-Yang came from the observation of nature and the environment. "Yin" originally referred to the shady side of a slope while "Yang" referred to the sunny side. Ancient Chinese people believed Yin was the north of mountain and south of water, while Yang was by the south of mountain and north of water. Many ancient cities' names derived from this concept, such as Luoyang city is to the north of the Luo

Yin-Yang is one of the dominate concepts in Chinese philosophy

river; Huaiyin city is to the south of the Huai river; Hengyang city is to the south of the Heng Mountain and Huayin city is to the north of the Hua mountain.

Later, this thinking was used in understanding other occurrences, which occurred in pairs and had complementary and opposing characteristics in nature. Some examples include: sky and earth, day and night, water and fire, active and passive, male and female and so on. Working with these ideas, ancient people recognized nearly all things could have Yin and Yang properties. Yin and Yang can describe two relative aspects of the same phenomena such as the example of the slope, or they can describe two different objects like sky and earth.

Usually, Yang is associated with energetic qualities. For example, movement, outward and upward direction, heat, brightness, stimulation, activity and excitement are all Yang qualities. Yin, on the other hand, is associated with the physical form of an object and has less energetic qualities such as rest, inward and downward direction, cold, darkness, condensation, inhibition, and nourishment.

Feng Shui

Feng Shui is an ancient Chinese system of aesthetics developed over 3,000 years ago. It is a complex body of knowledge that reveals how to balance the energies of any given space to ensure the health and good fortune of the people inhabiting it.

The words Feng Shui literally translate to "wind-water" in English. It is believed to utilize the laws of both heaven (astronomy) and earth (geography) to help one improve life by receiving positive "Qi". Qi rides the wind and scatters, but is retained when encountering water. It is either a movable positive or negative life force which plays an essential role in Feng Shui. In martial arts Qi refers to internal or physical energy. A traditional explanation of Qi as it relates to Feng Shui would include the orientation of a structure, its age, and its interaction with the surrounding environment including the local microclimates, the slope of the land, vegetation, and soil quality.

Feng Shui is all about the way that we live in harmony with the nature, benefiting from the positive energies in our living environment. By enhancing the relationship between people and their environment we find that the correct combination will create an ability to absorb the Qi or cosmic energy.

Traditional Feng Shui practice always requires an extremely accurate Chinese compass (Luo Pan), in order to determine the compass directions

Taiji and Bagua map

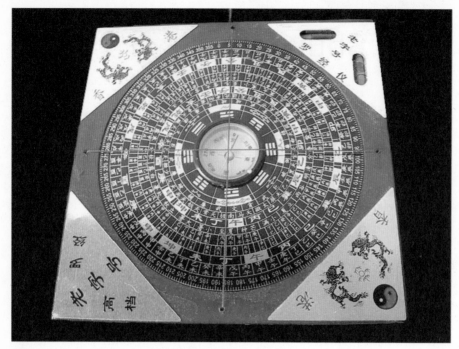

Chinese compass (Luo pan) used in divination

and find auspicious areas. Traditional Feng Shui also requires the calculation of a location's life force energy or Qi Level. When choosing a living environment, Feng Shui practitioners often consider the idea that a dwelling place should be surrounded by mountains and water, as well as gathering Qi. Good Feng Shui can be achieved by positioning furniture and fixtures at the appropriate places based on careful calculations to acheive the prefect overall balance of "Yin-Yang".

Feng Shui is an old Chinese art and science that is now becoming recognized by Western Cultures. It's an art similar to interior design in that it requires skill and knowledge, but also a science.

043

Twelve Zodiac Animals

The Chinese Lunar Calendar is based on the cycles of the moon, and is constructed in a different fashion than the Western solar calendar. And, unlike the Western zodiac signs, which follow a monthly cycle, the Chinese zodiacs follow a 12-year cycle, which is used for dating the years. They represent the Eastern cyclical concept of time, rather than the Western linear concept of time.

The Chinese animal zodiac is a rotating cycle of 12 animals, a different one for each year, and each animal has a different personality and different characteristics. The zodiac animal is believed to be the main contributing factor in personality traits, success, and happiness in a person's lifetime.

The sequence of animals goes according to a Chinese legend. The twelve animals quarreled one day as to who was to head the cycle of years. The gods were asked to decide, and they held a race to the opposite bank of the river. The order the animals finished in would determine the order of the zodiac signs. All the animals gathered at the riverbank and jumped in. Unbeknownst to the ox, the rat jumped on his back. As the ox was about to reach the shore, the rat jumped off of the ox's back onto the bank, and won the race. The pig, who was very lazy, ended up last. That is why the rat is the first year of the animal cycle, the ox second, and the pig last.

For a long time there has been a special relationship between humans and the twelve zodiacal animals. Humans admire them, take them as totems, and in the art world, the animal signs are frequent themes. This is often reflected in artisans' paper-cut works, New Year pictures, pottery and bronze wares. Especially noteworthy are early bronze mirrors that existed before the appearance of glass ones, on which elaborate zodiac animal depictions showed creativity and passion, and offered wishes for a good life.

Paper-cuttings about twelve zodiac animals

People under the rat sign are usually smart and willing to accumulate wealth and to make efforts to be successful. People born in ox year are probably honest, hardworking, patient, obstinate, and poor at communication. People born in the year of the tiger are tolerant, staunch, valiant and respected. The rabbit has represented hope to the Chinese people for a long time. People born under the sign of the rabbit are gentle, sensitive, modest and merciful and have strong memory. People under the sign of the dragon are lively, energetic and fortunate. They often can be leaders and try to go for perfection. Those born under the sign of the snake are seductive, gregarious, introverted, generous and charming. The horse people are born capable of quick action. They have a lively, sunny character. Lamb people are very patient. They are also very much self-motivated. Monkeys have a clear and precise mind. They think things over and are quick in action. Roosters have an active mind. But they are too impatient. They have an intense love of beauty. People born in the year of the dog respect and esteem their elders and teachers. Pigs have fortitude and are good leaders. They are mature and stable in handling things.

044

Chinese Lucky Numbers

Westerners might be a little curious as to why the 2008 Beijing Olympics started at 8 p.m. on August 8th. Generally speaking, it is connected closely with the Chinese belief in lucky numbers. Numbers play a significant role in Chinese culture, as the belief that certain numbers are lucky or unlucky is very strong.

In Chinese culture, lucky numbers always have a similar sound to an auspicious word. The numbers 6, 8 and 9 are considered lucky, so for important events people choose dates that contain these numbers. According to custom, odd numbers symbolize the bright male "yang" energy force, and even numbers represent the dark, undefined female "yin" force.

The number 1 represents honor, leadership and permanent development. 2 means to double, and is the number of cooperation and balance between yin and yang, or man and woman. A popular Chinese saying is "happiness comes as two."

The number 4(四 sì) sounds similar to the word for death(死 sǐ), hence it is considered very unlucky. 5 is popular in Chinese culture because of the five philosophical elements - water, metal, wood, fire and earth. There are also five blessings - longevity, prosperity, health, a virtuous life and natural death.

The pronunciation of 6 in Chinese sounds similar to the word for prosperity and hence is a very lucky number. You will be surprised to find many different goods in Chinese shopping malls are priced at 168 yuan - in sequence, the numbers 1, 6 and 8, bring happiness because 1(一 yāo), 6(六 liù) and 8(八 bā) sound very similar to yaoliufa(要六发), which means "the straight way to prosperity."

The number 8 in Chinese sounds similar to that for "fa" (发fā) which means multiplication and wealth. 8 is the luckiest number of all. People like for everything that they do to contain 8, so including 8 in

Number 9 has a symbol for "a long time". In order to get this auspicious meaning, many couples married on 9th September 2009.

dates, phone numbers and countless other things is very popular. This is why the Beijing Olympic Games began on 8/8/2008 at 8 p.m. - it was considered an extremely lucky and symbolic start date. In addition, the Chinese pronunciation of 8 is "ba", so 88 could be read "baba", which sounds like "bye bye", and "88" is slang for "goodbye" online.

9 is the best number because it contains characteristics of all the others. 9 sounds like the word (久 jiǔ), which means "a long time", with connotations of "forever". To Chinese ancients, 9 was the largest number pertaining to human matters, as 10 and upwards belonged to heaven. The number 9 was therefore solely for the emperor's use, and if any court official was found to have nine dragons embroidered on his robes he was immediately sentenced to death, along with his entire family. There are 9,999 rooms in the Forbidden City and the line of knobs on any door - horizontal or vertical - numbers exactly 9.

Chinese Medicine

Chinese medicine, also known as Traditional Chinese Medicine, has been practiced in China for thousands of years. Historically, it has played an important role in the prevention and treatment of diseases in China. With its complete theoretical system, firm clinical foundations and significant therapeutic effects, it is widely used in China today. It is based on a pre-scientific paradigm of medicine includes a range of traditional medical practices, like many other Chinese sciences, defines data on the basis of the inductive and synthetic mode of cognition.

From its ancient roots, Chinese medicine has developed into several inseparable facets, which include acupuncture, herbal medicine, Tuina, dietary regulation, and therapeutic exercise, such as Qigong and Taiji. Chinese medicinal theory is extremely complex and originated thousands of years ago through meticulous observation of nature, the cosmos, and the human body. It places special emphasis on preventive therapy. Periods of great stress or seasonal change, for example, are especially advantageous times to receive treatments of acupuncture and herbal therapy.

The core difference between Western and Chinese medicine lies in their conceptualization of the human body. One concept is not better than the other; instead, the two offer different perspectives, each with its own validity and limitations. Western medicine approaches the human body from an

Medicine chest to keep Chinese herbal medicine

Pulse-reading

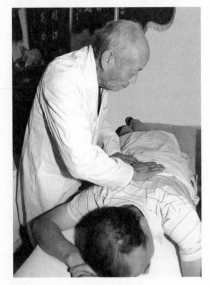

Tuina, a hands-on-body treatment in Chinese medicine.

anatomic and biochemical standpoint. It regards us as physical and biochemical beings made of many parts that can be dissected into tiny, independent components, and all internal changes can be expressed by biochemistry equation. Chinese medicine approaches the human body from an energetic and functional standpoint. It regards us as living organisms made of energetic, physical, emotional and spiritual parts that are intimately related.

Chinese medicine is considered to require considerable diagnostic skills. A training period of years or decades is said to be necessary for its practitioners to understand the full complexity of symptoms and dynamic balances. Following a macro philosophy of disease, traditional Chinese diagnostics are based on overall observation of human symptoms rather than micro level laboratory tests. There are four types of diagnostic methods: observation, hearing and smelling, asking about background and touching. The pulse-reading component of the touching examination is so important that Chinese patients may refer to going to the doctor as "going to have my pulse felt".

046

Chinese Acupuncture

Acupuncture is among the oldest healing practices in the world. As part of traditional Chinese medicine, acupuncture aims to relieve pain, maintain health and provide therapy through the stimulation of specific points on the body.

The term acupuncture describes a family of procedures involving the stimulation of anatomical points on the body using a variety of techniques. The acupuncture technique that has been most often studied scientifically involves penetrating the skin with thin, solid, metallic needles that are manipulated by hands or by electrical stimulation.

According to traditional Chinese medical theory, acupuncture points lie along meridians, where Qi, the body's energy flows. Health is a condition of balance of Yin and Yang within the body. Disease is due to an internal imbalance of Yin and Yang. An axiom of the medical literature of acupuncture is "no pain, no blockage; no blockage, no pain." Particularly important in acupuncture is the free flow of Qi.

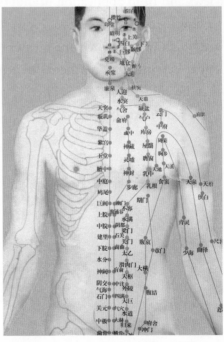

Approximately 2,000 years ago, the pre-eminent acupuncture text, *Huangdi Neijing (The Yellow Emperor's Classic on Internal Medicine)*, was written. In it, acupuncture was described as a means of letting out excess Qi or blood by making holes in the body along certain pathways,

Meridian-Collateral Diagram

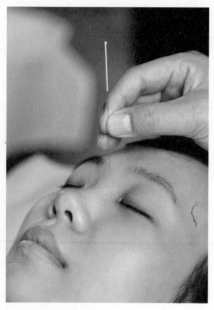

Acupuncture

called Jingluo (meridians). For some of these meridians, it was advised to acupuncture in such a way as to let out the blood but not the Qi; for others, to let out the Qi, but not the blood.

Many diseases were thought to enter the body through the skin, and then penetrate inward through muscle, internal organs, and, if not cured in timely fashion, to the marrow of the bone. By inserting a needle to the appropriate depth to correspond with the degree of disease penetration the disease could be let out.

The traditional and modern understandings of acupuncture arise from significantly different world views and from application of different levels of technology. It is difficult to directly correlate the two. However, modern studies have revealed that acupuncture stimulates one or more of the signaling systems, which can, under certain circumstances, increase the rate of healing response. This may be sufficient to cure disease, or to reduce its impact and alleviate some symptoms.

Chinese Materia Medica

Chinese materia medica (Zhong Yao), is the herbology based on traditional Chinese medicinal theory. As one of the most important components in traditional Chinese medicine, Chinese materia medica is an art of combining medicinal herbs. Each herbal medicine prescription is a cocktail of many herbs tailored to the individual patient. The practitioner usually designs a remedy using one or two main ingredients that target the illness. Then the practitioner adds many other ingredients to adjust the formula to the patient's Yin and Yang conditions. Sometimes, ingredients are needed to cancel out toxicity or side effects of the main ingredients. Some herbs require the use of other ingredients as a catalyst, or else the brew is ineffective. The latter steps require great experience and knowledge, and make the difference between a good Chinese herbal doctor and an amateur. Unlike Western medications,

Chinese herbal medicine

Chinese ginseng

Wolfberry

the balance and interaction of all the ingredients are considered more important than the effect of individual ingredients. A key to success in traditional Chinese medicine is the treatment of each patient as an individual.

Chinese herbology often incorporates ingredients from plants, animals and minerals sources. Plant sources are roots, stalks, bark, leaves, flowers, fruits and seeds of wild vegetation. Some can only be found in extreme climates and mountainous terrain. Animal sources include insects, marine animals and game. Mineral sources include crushed stones, fossilized bones and crushed shells. Most Chinese herbs are usually used to help build and strengthen the body. Traditionally, herbal remedies are mostly decocted into teas, to be taken warm, and are very bitter in taste. Some medicines are made from mixing ground herbs with honey to make herb pills.

Many of the modern day drugs have been developed from these herbs such as the treatments for asthma and hay fever from Chinese ephedra, hepatitis remedies from schizandra fruits and licorice roots and a number of anticancer agents from trees and shrubs. There are several herbal drugs that provide more energy, nourish the blood, calm tension and regulate bodily functions. There are over three hundred herbs that are commonly being used today that have a history that goes back at least 2,000 years.

Chinese Food Therapy

Chinese food therapy, also known as Chinese nutrition therapy, is the practice of healing using natural foods instead of medications. As one of the components of traditional Chinese medicine, food and medicine share much in common.

When treating sickness, Chinese doctors use herbal remedies initially to control the problem. They apply tried-and-true formulas with slight variations to meet the patient's specific conditions. Mixing herbs of similar properties increases the overall effectiveness. Mixing herbs of different properties can moderate the effects of the main herbs, complement the actions and minimize any adverse side effects. Some herbs can be as harsh as drugs, very forceful and effective, but are not to be taken continuously.

Various Chinese cereals and grains

Mutton for hotpot

Vegetables

Fruits

Chinese food therapy dates back as early as 2000 BC. When the Chinese discovered farming and agriculture, they discovered the medicinal properties of food. *The Yellow Emperor's Classic of Internal Medicine* also known as the *Huangdi Neijing*, was most important in forming the basis of Chinese food therapy. Since then, food has been studied and analyzed for its medicinal effects on people. This knowledge enables people to use food as the first line of defense to ward off common sicknesses and diseases. It is only when food alone cannot solve the health problem that people seek the help from medical practitioners.

Huangdi Neijing classified food by four food groups by their natures and characteristics. The four food groups in the Chinese diet are grains, fruits, meats and vegetables. Dairy products, especially cow's milk, are not considered suitable for humans. The *Huangdi Neijing* states that grains are for sustaining, vegetables are for filling, fruits are for supporting, and meats are for enhancing. Grains and vegetables are regarded as the basic foods necessary to sustain life. A balanced Chinese diet is 40 percent grains, 30 to 40 percent vegetables, 10 to 15 percent meats and the rest fruits and nuts.

Chinese Traditional Healthcare - The Health Preservation Theory

Health preservation is a concept in Chinese traditional medicine to enhance physical fitness, prevent diseases, postpone aging and prolong life. Healthcare includes spiritual toning, therapeutic diets and medicines, healthy exercises and other methods. These concepts' theoretical bases are closely tied to natural phenomena, and include the Five Elements Theory, Yin-Yang Theory, Pneumatism and Connecting with Macrocosm.

The ancients believed that all things in the world are generated from the five substances: metal, wood, water, fire and earth. This Five Element Theory also can be applied to explain the uniformity of mutual connection between human viscera and tissues as well as between human body and the external environment.

It has long been believed that all things in the world can be divided by Yin and Yang. If applied to medicine, Yin-Yang theory defines substances and functions that drive, warm and excite the human body as Yang, while such substances and functions that condense, moisturize and inhibit the human body are Yin. Yin and Yang rise and fall by restricting each other to achieve dynamic balance. If this balance is damaged, disease will manifest.

Therapeutic diets

Taiji

Five Elements Theory

The Qi is the source of changes of Yin and Yang and the Five Elements. Chinese medicinal theory states that man and nature communicate and correspond to each other. The theory of Pneuma and Man-Heaven Correspondence has been also applied to the understanding of human activities, as well as the explanation for the mutual restraint and effect of man and nature.

The concept of health preservation is the product of such natural views. It is in light of this concept that people established the rich and effective methods of health preservation, such as spiritual toning, guiding and breathing, healthcare according to the four seasons, and food and medicine diets for health preservation ,thus forming a miracle of the traditional Chinese medicine - Health Preservation Theory.

Four Treasures of the Study

In Chinese culture, the calligraphy brush, ink, paper and inkstone are the "Four Treasures of the Study". Despite the name, writing sets were often much more elaborate than these four items, containing many beautifully crafted tools. Scholars cherished their writing sets for the elegant style and exquisite craftwork. The materials of "Four Treasures of the Study" vary widely, from jade to bamboo. Generations of artisans have created these incredible and artistic tools with great skill and craftsmanship.

The writing brush is particular to China. The brushes vary, but white goat's hair, black rabbit's hair and yellow weasel's hair are the three major brush types. The brush handle can be made of common materials such as bamboo, wood, lacquer and porcelain, but can also be made of precious materials like pearl, ivory and jade.

Brushes

Brush pot, brush, ink stone, penholder, seal and seal box

Ink, often in the form of an ink stick, is the singular pigment used for Chinese calligraphy. It is made by burning pine or another wood in an earthenware container, mixing dense ash with oil and lacquer, and compressing it into an ink stick.

Paper is one of the most famous Chinese inventions. It is widely accepted that paper was invented by Cai Lun more than 1,800 years ago. In the Tang (618-907) and Song (960-1279) Dynasties, the paper producing industry thrived. In the Qing Dynasty (1644-1911), "Xuanzhi" was invented specifically for painting and calligraphy, and it is still used today. It is widely regarded as "the king of the paper".

The inkstone is the most important of "Four Treasures of the Study". Because of its durability, an inkstone can be passed down from ancient times. By mixing the ink stick with water, and then grinding it on the ink stone, the calligrapher or artist can create different opacities, textures and innumerable shades of black and gray ink.

The ancient tools of calligraphy not only included a brush, an ink stick, paper and an inkstone, but also accessories such as a penholder, a brush pot, an ink box, a paperweight, a seal and a seal box. The raw materials of these tools were usually pottery, porcelain, copper, iron, lacquer, wood, bamboo, stone, jade, agate and coral.

Go (Weiqi)

The game Go originated in China, and even has a longer history than Chinese chess which can date back to 2,500 years ago. In ancient times, it was a favorite game of the officers, scholars and noble ladies.

Go is a two-player game in which the players alternately place black and white stones. The one who controls a larger portion of the board at the end of the game wins. A stone or a group of stones is captured and removed if it has no empty adjacent intersections, and is completely surrounded by stones of the opposing color.

The board is marked with 19 horizontal lines and 19 vertical lines with 361 intersections. Both of the sides have 180 stone pieces, one with black and the other white. Placing stones close together helps them support each other and avoid capture. On the other hand, placing stones far apart creates influence across more of the board. Part of the strategic difficulty of the game stems from finding a balance between such conflicting interests. Players strive to serve both defensive and offensive purposes and choose between tactical urgency and strategic plans.

It is a tense game and the situation keeps changing. Playing Go can exercise one's brain and enhance logical thinking.

Weiqi

052

Chinese Painting

As opposed to Western painting, Chinese painting is also called "Guohua", which literally means national painting. Although it is one of the oldest artistic styles in the world, it began as ornamental embellishments on other art pieces, rather than stand-alone paintings. As early as in the Stone Age, Chinese pottery was painted with spirals, zigzags, dots, and animals. Not until 2,000 years ago, did Chinese artists begin to portray the world on a kind of silk.

Traditional Chinese painting involves essentially the same techniques as calligraphy and is accomplished with a brush dipped in black or colored ink; oils are not used. Just like calligraphy, the most popular materials on which paintings are made are paper and silk. The finished work is then fixed on scrolls, which can be hung or rolled up. Traditional painting is also done on albums and on walls, lacquer work, and other media.

Chinese painting

Chinese Painting《池塘清况》—Xie-yi, the works of modern artist—蒋山青 (Jiang Qingshan), collection of Tempo Arts.

Chinese Painting《觅》—Xie-yi, the works of modern artist—刘墨 (Liu Mo), collection of Tempo Arts.

The works of modern artist—范曾 (Fan Zheng), collection of Tempo Arts.

Chinese Painting 《孟蜀宫妓图》—Gong-bi , the works of a famous artist in Ming Dynasty—唐伯虎 (Tang Bohu 1470-1523), collection of the Palace Museum.

There are two main techniques in Chinese painting: Meticulous (Gong-bi), often referred to as "court-style" painting, and Freehand (Shui-mo) loosely termed water color or brush painting. This style is also referred to as "Xie-yi" or "freehand style".

Xie-yi, however, is the fundamental approach to Chinese painting that emphasizes the sentiment over realism. In their opinions, artists should not be restrained by reality, and paintings should serve as a means to convey how the artist looks at the world. In a word, traditional Chinese painters seek to portray a likeness in spirit rather than in appearance, because they are looking for the essence of an object. Guided by these theories, Chinese artists disregard the limitations of proportion, perspective, and light.

Traditional Chinese painting is a combination in the same picture of the arts of poetry, calligraphy, painting, and seal engraving. In ancient times most artists were poets and calligraphers. As for the Chinese, "painting in poetry and poetry in painting" has been one of the criteria for excellent works of art.

Peking Opera

With its fascinating and artistic accompanying music, singing and costumes, the Peking Opera is China's national opera. The opera presents the audience with an encyclopedia of Chinese culture, as well as unfolding stories, beautiful paintings, exquisite costumes, graceful gestures and martial arts.

In ancient times, Peking Opera was performed mostly on open air stages, teahouses or temple courtyards. Since the orchestra played loudly, the performers developed a piercing style of song that could be

Peking Opera

heard above the music. The costumes were a garish collection of sharply contrasting colors to stand out on dim stages illuminated only by oil lamps. Peking Opera is a harmonious combination of the Grand Opera, ballet and acrobatics, consisting of dance, dialogue, monologue, martial art and mime.

This special art derived from Chinese opera is rumored to have several different origins. But no matter its true origin, its signature, facial painting is worth appreciating for its artistic value. The paintings are representations of the characters' roles. For example, a red face usually depicts heroic bravery, uprightness and loyalty; a white face symbolizes a sinister, treacherous and insidious character; a green face connotes surly stubbornness, impetuosity and lack of self-restraint. In addition, facial painting patterns reveal information about a character as well. Essentially, the unique makeup allows characters on stage to reveal their characters voicelessly.

Peking Opera has a 200-year-long history. It is believed that Peking Opera gradually came into being after 1790 when the famous four Anhui opera troupes came to Beijing. Peking Opera underwent fast development during the reign of Emperor Qianlong and the notorious Empress Dowager Cixi under the imperial patronage, eventually becoming more accessible to the common people.

054

Calligraphy

Chinese calligraphy is one of the traditional arts that was once an important critical standard for Chinese literatis in the imperial era. Today it has spread not only throughout China, but also worldwide as a unique branch of art. The paper, ink, brush, and inkstone are essential implements of Chinese calligraphy. They are known together as the "Four Treasures of the Study" in China.

Calligraphy is so abstract and sublime that in Chinese culture it is universally regarded to be the most revealing symbol of a person. While one has conformed to the defined structure of words, the emotion and message of the calligraphy can be conveyed with great creativity by individuals.

In contrast to the Western calligraphy, diffuse ink blots and dry brush strokes are viewed as a natural and free impromptu expression. All the variations of calligraphy style depend on the mental focus that coordinates the mind and the body to choose the proper way to express the content of a passage.

Calligraphy—《兰亭序》 *Preface to the Poems Composed at the Orchid Pavilion*

Chinese Calligraphy

Chinese Calligraphy on spring couplets

To become an artist or expert in calligraphy, one has to practice word by word and stroke by stroke until each brushstroke has been ingrained in one's mind. Chinese calligraphy can temper a person into a state in which one can apply subconsciously control the concentration of ink and the compatibility of font and size of each piece or word. It is also considered an active way of keeping one fit and healthy, for the practice is relaxing and entertaining. Historically, many calligraphy artists were known for their longevity.

Kunqu

Kunqu opera is one of the oldest and most refined styles of traditional Chinese theatre still performed today, which can be traced back over 600 years. It is a synthesis of drama, opera, ballet, poetry recital, and musical recital, which also draws on earlier forms of Chinese theatrical performances.

Originating in the city of Kunshan, Suzhou, southeast China, Kunqu flourished during the Ming Dynasty (1368-1644). By the end of the 16th century, Kunqu spread from the Suzhou region to the rest of China, and for the next 200 years was the most prestigious form of Chinese drama. Kunqu boasts a 600-year history and is known as the "teacher" or "mother" of a hundred operas, because of its influence on other Chinese theatre forms, including Peking Opera.

Scene from The Peach Blossom Fan

Scene from The Peony Pavilion

The Kunqu opera is characterized by its dynamic structure and elegant music. When performed, the dialogue is interspersed with arias sung to traditional melodies, called Qupai. Each word or phrase is expressed by a stylized movement or gesture that is essentially part of a dance with strict rules of style and execution, much like classical ballet. Even casual gestures must be precisely executed and timed to coordinate with the music and percussion.

As in all traditional Chinese operas, Kunqu uses a minimum of props and scenery, which permits the performers to more easily express their stage movements in the form of dance. The performers appeal to

Scene from The Romance of the Western Bower

the audience's imagination and conjure up a scene or a setting (such as a door, a horse, a river, a boot) with words, gestures and music. The costumes are elaborately exaggerated versions of the dress style in the Ming Dynasty.

Today, Kunqu is performed professionally in China. It was listed as one of the Masterpieces of the Oral and Intangible Heritage of Humanity by UNESCO in 2001. Its melody or tune is one of the Four Great Characteristic Melodies in Chinese opera.

Chinese Tea

Chinese people are believed to have enjoyed tea drinking for more than 4,000 years. Tea - which is native to China - was originally used by the ancient Chinese for medical purposes. At that time, tealeaves were eaten, and later it was developed into the popular drink we now know as tea. Over many years, the Chinese learned to grow tea plants and use their leaves to make various types of tea.

The most prosperous era in the history of tea was the 7th century, when the influential book, *The Classic of Tea* by Chinese tea sage Luyu, appeared. This book detailed the history, rules and skills needed for tea drinking and cultivation in China.

Tea can be classified as green tea, black tea, oolong tea and scented tea, according to the processing method. Green tea is the most popular type of tea consumed in China. Well-known green teas include Longjing from the West Lake, Biluochun from Wu County, Jiangsu Province, Huangshan Maofeng from Mt. Huangshan in Anhui, and Junshan Silver from the Hills of Junshan, Dongting Lake, Hunan Province.

Tea plant

Tea pots and tea cups

Black tea is fermented tea. Unlike green tea, black tea does not lose its fragrance easily, so it is suitable for long-distance transportation. It is believed to warm the stomach and is good for drinking in autumn and winter. The most famous black teas include Qi Hong, Dian Hong and Ying Hong. Hong(红hóng) means red; black tea is called Hong Cha(红茶hóng chá), red tea, in Chinese.

Oolong tea is a semi-fermented tea, which is a mix between green tea and black tea. It is most known for the complexity of its brewing process and the highly ceremonial way of drinking it - it is often called Kung-fu tea(功夫茶gōng fu chá). Usually, drinking oolong tea requires a set of tea wares that includes a stove, teapot and tiny teacups. The three major oolong growth areas are Fujian, Guangdong, and Taiwan. Big red robe (大红袍dà hóng páo), and Tieguanyin are the most representative types of Oolong tea in China.

The standard Kung-fu tea ceremony requires intricate technique and many steps. The tea is often presented first, and before brewing the host goes through several steps of washing and heating the teapots and teacups with hot water. The leaves are steeped briefly, and the first pot of tea is discarded, after which the tea is steeped again and served quickly. The host must also wipe bubbles and spilled water off of the teapot. The technique is very important in a tea ceremony - the pouring heights are

A set of tea making wares

Tie Guan Yin(one kind of famous tea)

varied depending on the point in the ceremony and each step is completed with care. Generally, there are four people involved in a Kung-fu tea ceremony, including the host who serves the tea.

Dim sum is usually served alongside Chinese tea. These small snacks are usually served in a small steamer basket or on a small plate. Yum cha (literally "tea drinking") is the term used to describe the dining session, especially in contemporary Cantonese dining.

In China, hot tea is served for refreshment just as commonly Coca-Cola is served in America. However, a cup of hot tea may do more than just relax you. Research shows drinking tea may help prevent a wide range of ailments, such as high blood pressure, heart disease, Parkinson's Disease and even cancer. More and more young people are beginning to drink tea, as it can also help lose weight healthily.

Chinese Knots

Chinese knot, (Zhong Guo Jie) is a traditional, decorative handicraft in China. It's woven from one piece of thread and named according to its shape and meaning. In Chinese, "Jie" (结) means reunion, friendliness, peace, warmth, marriage and love. Chinese knots are often used to express good wishes for happiness, prosperity, love and protection from evil.

Chinese people have known how to tie decorative knots for thousands of years. As civilization advanced, Chinese people used knots for more than just fastening

Two girls are tying Chinese knot.

and wrapping. Some knots were used to record events, while others had a purely ornamental function.

Every basic knot is named after either its outer form or the practical use. The Two-Coins Knot, for example, is shaped like two overlapping coins once used in ancient China. The Button Knot functions as a button.

Today, Chinese knots have expanded in function and widened in application. Jewelry, clothing, gift-wrapping and furniture can be accentuated with unique Chinese knots. Large Chinese knot wall hangings have the same decorative value as fine paintings or photographs.

The Chinese knot, with its classic elegance and ever-expanding variation, is both practical and ornamental, reflecting the grace and depth of Chinese culture.

Chinese knot

Quietly, Chinese trends have swept the entire world. We can often see women from Western countries, with their gingery hair and blue eyes, wearing a traditional Chinese-style dress, such as a Cheongsam with knots on it. These exquisitely symmetrical knots, which serve as adornments all over the world, are as complex as the cultural heritage of the Chinese people.

058

Cheongsam

The cheongsam is a dress with distinctive Chinese features that is enjoying growing popularity in the international world of high fashion.

The name "cheongsam", meaning simply "long dress", entered the English vocabulary from the dialect of China's Guangdong Province (Cantonese). In other parts of the country including Beijing, however, it is known as "qipao", which has an interesting history behind it.

When the early Manchu rulers came to China proper, they organized certain people, mainly Manchus, into "banners" (qi) and called them "banner people" (qiren), which then became loosely the name of all Manchus. The Manchu women wore normally a one-piece dress, which likewise came to be called "qipao" or "banner dress". Although the 1911 Revolution toppled the rule of the Qing (Manchu) Dynasty, the dress survived the political change and, with later improvements, has become the traditional dress for Chinese women.

During the 1920s, the Han people incorporated some Western cloth-making techniques into making the dress, making it more like an evening gown worn by Western women. It soon became the most fashionable attire in Shanghai. With its form-fitting shape, many Chinese women liked to wear it. As time went by, the dress went through more changes, and it became a must for all Chinese women during the 1930s. At that time, many famous film actresses also wore cheongsam, which made them even more popular.

Easy to slip on and comfortable to wear, the cheongsam fits the female Chinese figure well. Its neck is

Buttons on cheongsam

A woman in Cheongsam

high with a closed collar, and its sleeves may be short, medium or full length, depending on season and taste. The dress is buttoned on the right side, with a loose bosom, a close-fitting waist, and slits up the sides, all of which combine to highlight the beauty of the female form.

Cheongsam

The cheongsam is not too complicated to make, nor does it call for too much material, since there are no accessories like belts, scarves, sashes or frills to on it.

Another beauty of the cheongsam is that, made of different materials and to varying lengths, they can be worn either on casual or formal occasions. In either case, it creates an impression of simple and quiet charm, elegance and neatness. No wonder it is so well liked by women not only of China but of foreign countries as well.

Cheongsam has been experiencing constant changes as trends change with the times. While inheriting the characteristics of traditional cheongsam in details, new cheongsams feature a great deal of modern design elements in color, cut and style. Most notably, the skirts now come in A-line, asymmetrical and picture puzzle cuts, and the skirts now feature diversified materials. Other than meeting aesthetic requirements of young women in China, the new-style cheongsam is of great versatility with its ease of wearing.

In the 2008 Summer Olympics, cheongsams were the uniforms for the medal bearers. They were also worn by female members of the Swedish team in the opening ceremony, designed in Sweden's national colors of blue and yellow.

059

Chopsticks

Chopsticks(筷子Kuàizi) are the most common utensils for Chinese. They are a pair of small, tapered sticks of equal length, made of bamboo, plastic, metal or wood. It is common knowledge that the Chinese invented chopsticks, and as early as the Shang dynasty chopsticks were widely used throughout East Asia. With the influx of Chinese immigrants in Southeast Asia, in the past several hundred years the use of chopsticks has spread to other Asian countries like Japan, Korea and Vietnam.

Chinese food is always chopped into bite size when it is served. One reason is that small pieces are more convenient for people to use chopsticks to pick up. For another reason, it is forbidden in Chinese culture to use instruments for slaughtering livestock at the dinning table,

Chopsticks

---

making knives off-limits. Under the influence of Confucianism, the Chinese see the knife and fork as symbols of violence. Chopsticks, on the other hand, are seen as reflecting gentleness and benevolence.

Chopsticks are maneuvered in one hand, between the thumb and fingers, and used to pick up pieces of food. It may be hard for Westerners to use two slim and slippery sticks to pick up grains of rice and small pieces of meat and vegetables, but practice makes perfect. To use chopsticks, hold one chopstick in place between your thumb and index finger, and pivot the other one with your fingertips to pick up a morsel.

It is important to follow basic chopstick etiquette when dining with Chinese friends or business partners. Chopsticks are not used to toy with one's food or with communal dishes. Chopsticks should not be used to make noise or to draw attention to something. It also is poor etiquette to tap chopsticks on the edge of one's bowl.

Ancient Chinese people believed that a person's hands were closely connected with their mind, and that using chopsticks could greatly increase the fingers' flexibility, and thus enhance one's intelligence. In fact, scientists have found that the human brain can be stimulated through frequent finger movement. When using chopsticks, one has to coordinate the thumb, forefinger, palm and middle finger, all requiring an active mind. Now, many parents start their children using chopsticks at an early age, giving their brains extra stimulation, and hopefully giving them some extra smarts.

The correct way of using Chopsticks

060

Chinese Family Value

When it comes to Chinese family values, the most distinguished feature is the attention to "Xiao" (孝) which means "filial piety".

Filial piety is a concept originating with Confucianism. The term "filial piety" refers to the extreme respect that Chinese children are supposed to show their parents. It involves many different things, including taking care of parents, burying them properly after death, bringing honor to the family, and having a male heir to carry on the family name. Practicing these ideals is a very important part of Chinese culture. Therefore, as one would expect, filial piety has been incorporated into the major beliefs systems of China.

Filial piety exists today and can be seen in China, as well as outside of it. Many Chinese immigrant families all over the world live in multi-generational family units. It is never "okay" to abandon older family members. Older generations often form a very important part of day-to-day living. Since in both China and in the US, both members of a married couple may work, care of the children is needed. The mother of either the husband or wife frequently provides that care. This keeps the notion of filial piety strong. The older parent continues to contribute to the adult children's and grandchildren's well being.

What are some results of filial piety? Here are some ways it can show itself today:

You feel you have a life-long duty to please your parents.

You feel a strong obligation to fulfill your parents' expectations about your studies and career.

You are not truly successful unless your achievements are appreciated by your parents.

Your parents' expectations and your desire for their approval motivate your pursuit of success.

A Chinese woman and her mother

If you fail a subject, you would be more worried about your parents being disappointed than your own pride.

If your father committed a crime, you would not feel guilty concealing it from the police.

It means more to you than anything else that your parents think of you as a good son or daughter.

061

Chinese Rites

As China is known as the "Land of Ceremony and Propriety", Chinese rites range widely in form and function. They are an integral part of daily life as well as all important holidays and ceremonies, which are all equipped with detailed etiquette standards. These rigorous and wide-ranging standards of ritual and etiquette are known as "Li".

A sophisticated system of Li came into being in the Zhou Dynasty, so as to regulate people's conduct, reconcile conflicts, coordinate interpersonal relationships and ensure perfect management of personnel affairs through implementation of specific regulations. Li enforces social order, puts an end to conflicts and the scourge of war, and moderates extravagance. Li is seen as the basis of people's happiness in their personal lives and work.

Li is the desirable standard of conduct advocated by Confucius. During the Confucian period, people had gradually drifted away from the rites of the Zhou, prompting Confucius to begin advocating the practice of Li once more.

Adult ceremony for boys in Ancient China

In daily life, people are expected to be filial to parents, kind to children, respectful to elder brothers, harmonious with their spouse, courteous to friends and helpful to neighbors. Chinese etiquette demands that one be polite and deferential to others, while obeying social rules and managing affairs appropriately. These Chinese rites have had a long standing and close link to politics. From ancient times onward, practicing Li was not only a virtue, but vital to one's success as well. After Confucius' time, Li was stressed to enhance ethics, morality and social order.

Li stands for a complex set of ideas that is difficult to explain in Western languages. There is an essential difference between Western and Eastern societies when it comes to law, etiquette and ritualism. Confucius argues that under law, external authorities administer punishments after illegal actions, so people generally behave well without understanding reasons why they should. But more effectively, with strong rituals, patterns of behavior are internalized and exert their influence before actions are taken, so people behave properly because they fear shame and want to avoid losing face.

Ritual can be seen as a means to finding the balance between opposing qualities that might otherwise lead to conflicts. Ritual divides people into categories and builds hierarchical relationships through protocol and ceremonies, assigning everyone a place in society and a code of behavior. In Chinese society, obeying rituals with sincerity is the most powerful way to cultivate oneself.

062

Delicious Chinese Cuisine

Chinese cuisine enjoys worldwide renown for its complex techniques, variety of ingredients and seasonings, and its balance between flavor and nutrition. Chinese dishes are exquisite and well-designed. Since China is so large, the flavor of food varies from area to area. Southerners like light flavors, while northerners prefer heavily seasoned dishes. Sichuan people like spicy food and Shan'xi people like sour food.

Staple foods include steamed buns(Baozi), dumplings(Jiaozi), noodles(Miantiao) and rice. China has many regional specialties and snacks. The southerners prefer rice, while the northerners prefer noodles. Beijing cuisine is famous for roasted duck, Guangdong snacks are similar to Western snacks, and Suzhou snacks have pleasant colors and beautiful shapes. The most famous Chinese regional specialties include bean curd jelly from Beijing, Goubuli steamed buns from Tianjin, and small

Rice is one of the most popular staple food in China

Noodles

Cantonese snacks

Roast duck is a popular dish
for foreigners

steamed pork buns served in steamer trays and dumplings stuffed with crab meat, sesame paste and pea sprouts from Shanghai.

Generally speaking, there are eight regional cuisines in China. The style of Lu (Shandong) is the largest due to its long history. The other three largest cuisines are Su (named after Jiangsu's major style, Huaiyang cuisine), Chuan (from Sichuan) and Yue (from Guangdong).

Chinese cuisine seeks harmony in the integration of color, aroma, taste, shape and ingredient quality. Among the many cooking methods Chinese cooking uses are boiling, stewing, braising, frying, steaming, baking and simmering.

063

Chinese Food: Art of Culinary

Chinese cooking embodies the food culture tradition of Chinese nation. It has many distinctive features.

1. Fine Slicing Techniques

Slicing technique is namely the cutting treatment of a chef on raw materials of food so that the materials might have an orderly and identical shape required by cooking. In this way, the materials become tasty while retaining certain structural beauty. Through repeated practice, chefs of past dynasties have created abundant ways of cutting, such as straight cutting, slice cutting, oblique cutting, score cutting (scoring the material without cutting off) and engraving cutting, processing raw materials into all shapes such as slices, strips, shreds, pieces, diamonds, granules, pastes, and into a variety of designs and colors such as "pellet", "ball", "ear of wheat", "raincoat", "orchid" and "chrysanthemum".

2. Five Flavors in Harmonious Proportion

Flavoring is an important cooking technique. A Chinese saying says, "If five flavors are in harmonious proportion, there will be a hundred sweet-smelling flavors." The flavors of fish and meat dishes are divided into the basic type and the compound type. The basic type is probably divided into nine categories, namely, saltiness, sweetness, sourness, spiciness, bitterness, freshness, fragrance, numbness and lightness.

3. Emphasis on Aesthetic Feeling

Chinese cooking has traditionally placed an emphasis on the aesthetic feeling of dishes and

Delicate food cutting technique

Delicate food cutting technique

seeks for harmony of the food's color, fragrance, flavor, shape and utility. Whether it is a red radish or a green cabbage, all kind of designs can be carved out, which gives a unique style, attains the harmony of color, fragrance, flavor, shape and beauty and provides people with highly unified special enjoyment in spirit and material.

4. Seeking for Health

The cooking techniques of our country are closely related to Chinese medical treatment and healthcare. We believe that food and traditional medicine have the same origin and uses. We can take advantage of the medicinal properties of the raw ingredients and turn them into all kinds of food, thereby accomplishing the purpose of preventing and curing certain diseases.

064

Sichuan Cuisine

Since China covers a large territory, Chinese food differs greatly. It can be roughly divided into eight regional cuisines, each with its own distinctive features. Among them, Sichuan cuisine is perhaps the most popular. Originating in Sichuan Province of southwestern China, it is famed for its spicy dishes, in particular its unique use of local chili peppers that numb the tongue. However, Sichuan cuisine boasts a variety of flavors and methods of cooking according to different regions.

Steamed Fish Head with Diced Hot Red Peppers

Mapo Tofu

The earliest history can be traced back to between 221 BC and AD 220, when Sichuan cuisine developed a distinctive flavor. It is recorded that 800 years ago, Sichuan cuisine was extremely popular and Sichuan restaurants were opened in the capital. The hot pepper was introduced to China from South America around the end of the 17th Century. Once it came to Sichuan, it became very popular in their dishes. In the late Qing Dynasty around 19th Century, Sichuan cuisine became recognized as its own unique brand of Chinese cuisine, enjoying the same reputation and status as Shandong, Guangdong (Canton) and Huaiyang cuisines.

Sichuan cuisine got its reputation from its spicy flavor. The local chili and red peppers likely contributed much to its red-hot reputation. In ancient times when it was very humid and rainy, local people used red peppers as a kind of Chinese medicine to reduce internal dampness.

Due to Sichuan's warm and humid climate, Sichuan cuisine also uses a lot of preserved foods, including pickled, salted, dried and smoked foods. As a result, Sichuan chefs are good at cooking dry and preserved food dishes. On the downside, even today many Sichuan cooks still have a hard time cooking Sichuan dishes using fresh foods, such as seafood.

Typical cooking methods of Sichuan cuisine include stir-frying, steaming and braising. Famous dishes from Sichuan include Twice-

Boiled Fish with Bean Sprouts in Hot Chili Oil   Beef in Chili Sauce

cooked Pork, Kung Pao Chicken, and Shredded Pork in Garlic Sauce. One of the most popular dishes is Mapo Tofu, which was invented by a Chengdu, Sichuan chef's pockmarked wife decades ago in the Qing Dynasty. The cubed tofu is cooked over a low flame in a sauce that contains ground beef, chili, and peppercorns. When served, the tofu is tender, spicy, and delicious.

Cantonese Cuisine

Almost as popular as Sichuan cuisine in China and abroad, Cantonese cuisine comes from Guangdong Province in southern China, specifically from its capital city, Guangzhou. Of all the regional varieties of Chinese cuisine, Cantonese is perhaps most popular among Westerners, as many Chinese restaurants in Chinatowns across the world serve Cantonese cuisine.

Cantonese cuisine is especially famed for its diversity of ingredients. Cantonese cooks also use a variety of cooking methods, including steaming, stir-frying, shallow-frying, double-boiling, braising, and deep-frying.

Cantonese cuisine is much lighter in flavor than other regional cuisines in China. However, this doesn't mean it lacks in flavor, as Cantonese cooks focus on accentuating the natural flavors of fresh ingredients without over seasoning dishes. As a result, Cantonese food tends to be more nutritious and healthy.

Different kinds of Cantonese dim sum

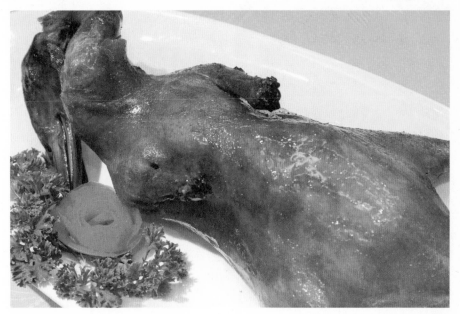

Cantonese roast duck

Light seasonings such as spring onions, sugar, salt, soy sauce, rice wine, cornstarch, vinegar, sesame oil, and other oils suffice to enhance flavor in most Cantonese cooking. While ginger, chili peppers, five-spice powder, white pepper powder and star anise are used sparingly.

The most popular Cantonese dishes include Chinese steamed eggs(Zheng Dan), Sweet and sour pork(Gu Lao Rou), Cantonese fried rice(Chao Fan) and Wonton soup(Hun Tun). While many of these are on the menus of typical Cantonese restaurants, others are more commonly found in Chinese homes due to their simplicity. Homemade Cantonese dishes are usually served with plain white rice.

Another notable Cantonese specialty is slow-cooked soup, usually cooked with the clay pot. The soup is usually a clear broth prepared by simmering meat and other ingredients for several hours. Sometimes, Chinese herbal medicines are added to the pot. There are hundreds of recipes of the soup. The turtle soup, pigeon soup, the abalone soup are most popular, but usually soups consist of a mixture of vegetables and

Fuo Tiao Qiang

Slow-cooked soup

bones. Other ingredients include ginger, dates and herbal medicines. The highlight of Cantonese soups is the fragrant broth, although of course the chunky parts of the soup are delicious as well.

Without a doubt, dim sum is the trademark food of Cantonese cuisine. It is usually eaten in the morning and afternoon. Dim sum is a delectable array of little snacks, which come in bamboo baskets that are placed on trolleys, and pushed around by waiters or waitresses for costumers to order. The most popular dim sum items are shrimp dumplings, prawn and pork dumplings, steamed spareribs, spring rolls and steamed barbecued pork buns.

Cooking Methods of Chinese Food

Cooking techniques are almost the recipe in Chinese Cuisine. Cooking temperatures and cooking methods are as important as the ingredients that form the dish. Each technique is chosen carefully. The nature of the ingredients, the degree of heat, and timing are considered; certain techniques seal in juices, while others importantly affect flavor.

1. Stir-frying - Chao (炒)

Stir-frying is the classic Chinese cooking method. In this method, the chef quickly cooks the food over high heat in a small amount of oil, tossing and turning the food as it cooks. In stir-frying, the food should always be in motion. Spread it around the pan or up the sides of the wok, then toss it together again in the center and repeat. This method allows meats to stay juicy and flavorful, vegetables to come out tender-crisp.

Stir-frying

Steamed fish

Braised pork with soy sauce

2. Deep-frying - Zha (炸)

Deep-frying is another common method of Chinese food preparation. Certain main dishes also call for meats to be deep-fried for a crunchy coating, then stir-fried to combine them with vegetables and flavorings. The oil must be at the right temperature (360℃ to 375℃) to cook food properly. If it sizzles and skates around the surface of the oil, the temperature is right. If it sinks, the oil is not hot enough. If it browns too quickly, and the oil smokes, the temperature is too high. Oil can be reduced if you strain it and add fresh oil each time. Keep a separate batch for frying fish and seafood.

3. Steaming - Qing Zheng (清蒸)

Steaming preserves flavors and food nutrients through the use of steam temperature rather than higher temperatures that destroy or leach these nutrients in discarded boiling water. All sorts of foods are steamed: meat, fish, dumplings, buns stuffed with meat or a sweet bean paste-bread. For best results, the water should be boiling when the food goes into the steamer and the flame should be high enough to keep it boiling.

4. Braising - Hong Shao (红烧)

Braising is uniquely Chinese, here the food is cooked in large quantities of soy sauce and water rather than in water alone. The soy sauce makes the dish rich, tasty, and reddish brown. It is usually made of pork, beef, ham, chicken, duck, or carp. It is used primarily for cooking meats. Vegetables, if included, are added later just before serving or towards the end of cooking. Various seasonings, flavors and condiments are added to red-stewed dishes such as soy, sherry, ginger, scallions, cilantro and many more.

067

Chinese Food: Ingredient Selection

Chinese cuisine is most well known for its various flavors and ingredients. There is an old saying "Anything that walks, swims, crawls, or flies with its back to heaven is edible." It is not surprising that nearly everything can be used in Chinese cuisine. In addition, there are some ingredients that sound exotic to foreigners. Fowl organs, animal heads and feet, snakes, and insects are cooked in various ways to appeal to people's taste.

However, that's only small part of Chinese food. Ingredient selection is the first and foremost technique for Chinese chefs, and the basis for making top grade Chinese cuisine. It requires rich knowledge and skilled techniques.

Beijing Roast Duck

West Lake Fish in Vinegar Gravy

Bamboo shoots

The raw materials of each cuisine include main ingredients, side ingredients, supplementary ingredients and seasonings, which all need careful study and have fixed patterns. They can be generalized as the two words of "exquisiteness" and "fineness". This is what Confucius says of high quality ingredients and finely cut meat. "Exquisiteness" means when selecting ingredients, people should consider their characteristics, for example places of origin, seasons and growth period.

Superior materials should be fresh, rich, tender, and excellent in quality. Take Beijing roasted duck as example. It selects the "stuffed duck" produced in Beijing. An excellent quality duck has a weight around two and a half kilograms. If it is too large, the flesh will be old, while if it is too small, the flesh will not be fatty and delicious enough. Sometimes ingredients need special treatment according to the flavor of dishes. Take the famous dish of Hangzhou "West Lake fish in vinegar" as example. It selects live grass carp produced by the West Lake. Though it tastes fresh, it has loose flesh and the smell of earth. Therefore, it should be placed in a specially made bamboo cage and starved for two days in clear water until its flesh becomes solid and the odor of earth is got rid of. In this way, the fish will taste more tender and delicious with the flavor of crab flesh after being cooked. "Fineness" means selecting raw ingredients from the best part of the plant or animal. For example, the famous cuisine "chicken cubes with peanuts" selects the tender flesh at the breast of a spring chicken of the same year so as to guarantee the tenderness of flesh.

068

The Art of Dining, Chinese Style

Eating is an essential part of the Chinese culture. In fact, much of Chinese life centers around food. It has even been said that Chinese people eat everything with four legs except the table. It should not be surprising that there are many Chinese customs relating to dining and eating. Chinese children are taught traditional eating habits and eating patterns from a young age.

Chinese prefer round dining tables because more people can be seated around the table. A round table allows people to eat facing each other without differentiation. In other words, when seated at a round table everyone is equal, regardless of their social status or wealth.

Meal time is a time for family members to converse. The dining table is a place for discussing business, education and other interesting and important topics. Discussing gloomy matters such as death, accidents and other misfortunes is regarded as bad table manners.

Chinese people prefer round dining tables.

Chinese Liquor

It is customary for a bowl of soup to be placed in the center of the table. Soup is believed to be nutritious and a good source of energy. Spoons are provided for each person to share the soup. Other dishes such as fish, vegetables, meat and eggs are placed around the table.

The main difference between Chinese and western eating habits is that unlike the West, where everyone has their own plate of food, in China the dishes are placed on the table and everybody shares from the communal plates. If you are being treated by a Chinese host, be prepared to eat a ton of food. The Chinese are very proud of their culture of cuisine and will do their best to show their hospitality by serving elaborate meals.

Sometimes, the Chinese host will even use their chopsticks to put food in your bowl or plate. In China, this is a sign of politeness, and your hosts will often encourage you to eat more. The appropriate thing to do is to eat the whatever it is and say how great it is. If you feel uncomfortable with this, you can just say a polite thank you and leave the food there.

Chinese Etiquette in Dining With Guests

Few, if any, countries in the world have a richer culinary tradition than China. Indeed, Chinese food is available - and popular - in nearly every country on earth. There is much more to Chinese food than just its rich diversity of dishes. As important as any ingredient or cooking style is the concept of face.

What and how much hosts order for guests are generally taken as a reflection of regard in which the host holds the guest. Chinese hosts tend, therefore, to order high quality dishes and in great quantity. On many occasions, Chinese hosts invite guests to dinner, saying, "Just order what you like. This dinner is very informal." whereupon the guests have ordered things like kung-pao chicken, home-style tofu, or spinach with

A Chinese dining party

garlic, a few very simple dishes. The host would then laugh and say, "No, no. How about some steamed crab or prawns? Maybe fish." To the Chinese mind, if the host were to order the dishes the guests suggested, he/she would lose face.

Quantity is equally important. Chinese tend to order - and in their own homes - prepare much, much more food than the number of people attending can reasonably be expected to eat. When there is a lot of food left over at the end of the meal, the host can be assured that she had ordered a sufficient quantity. Of course, over the years, this practice has resulted in an incalculable amount of wasted food, though, thankfully, the trend in recent years seems to be toward taking food home. But the persistence of this emphasis on quantity bespeaks the continued importance of considerations of face.

Finally, there is the question of paying the bill. When the roles of host and guest are clearly defined, as is always the case on formal occasions, this isn't an issue. The hosts typically remain on for a few minutes after the guests have departed and pay the bill. When the occasion is less formal, however, such as when a few friends get together for a meal, the payment of the bill becomes a matter of face. As the bill is brought to the table, one or more of the persons attending the dinner will insist on paying it. People may have seen two friends struggle so aggressively to pay the bill, each pulling money from the pocket and pushing back the outstretched arm of the other, that an onlooker could have easily mistaken the scene for a fist fight. This type of scene is commonplace in restaurants across the country, another striking testament to the importance of face in the context of dining.

Eating in Chinese Restaurants

Tea is usually served as soon as you have a seat in a Chinese restaurant. The server serves you tea while you read the menu and decide what to order. The teapot is left on the table after every customer's cup has been filled with tea, so that you may serve yourself when you need more. When the server pours tea in a customer's cup, he or she often taps the table with his or her index and middle fingers for two or three times, which is a way of thanking the server and to signal that they have enough tea. The server will stop pouring after seeing this gesture.

Eating Ambience

If you like to bring a book to dinner, look elsewhere - Chinese restaurants are usually filled with raucous conversation and laughter. People like to let loose when having a gathering, and meals are no exception. As a rule, Chinese people judge a restaurant's dishes based on whether the restaurant is noisy or not, because a crowd at a restaurant indicates its dishes are delicious. If you want a quiet place to enjoy your meals, restaurants also provide small, private rooms, which Chinese people call "Bao Jian".

Bao Jian inside

Menu Translation

Many Chinese dishes are translated word for word, and thus make westerners confused and even scared. For example,

Eating in a Chinese restaurant

westerners may feel horrible when they see "red burned lion head" (红烧狮子头) on the menu. But actually, this creatively named dish consists of freshly stewed pork balls that look like a lion's head.

Mapo tofu is often translated as bean curd made by a pock-marked woman, but in fact it is a popular Sichuan cuisine dish consisting of bean curd with spicy minced pork. Unfortunately, some people may be misled by the translation, and miss this delicious dish. One of the most terrifying dishes is "husband and wife's lung slice". However it is one of the most popular dishes in Chinese restaurants, and should be translated as beef in chili sauce.

Seating Arrangements in China

China is a nation mindful of etiquette, particularly when it comes to food, which has been an important part of the culture since antiquity. Dining etiquette has naturally become an important part of dining culture, and the seating arrangement is the most important feature of Chinese dining etiquette.

From ancient times to the present, as the evolution of dining furniture progressed, the arrangement of seats changed accordingly. In general, the seats on the left and facing the east, or the entrance gate is the seat of honor. The seat of honor in a family banquet is reserved for the elder with the highest position in the family hierarchy, and the least prominent seat is taken by the person with the lowest position.

The seat in the central back is the seat of honor.

When a family holds a banquet with guests, the seat of honor is for the guest with the highest status and the host takes the least prominent seat. If the guest of honor is not seated, other people are not allowed to be seated. If he hasn't eaten, others should not begin to eat.

When taking rounds of drinks, people drink a toast from the seat of honor down to the least prominent seat in order.

If it is a round table, then the person facing the entrance is the guest of honor. The seats on the left hand are in turn second, fourth and sixth, while those on the right hand are in turn third, fifth and seventh, and so forth, until they join together.

If it is an Eight Immortals table and there is a seat facing the entrance, then the right-hand seat facing the door is for the guest of honor. If there is no seat facing the entrance, then the right-hand seat facing the east is the seat of honor. The seats on the left side of the seat of honor are the second, fourth, sixth and eighth, and those on the right side are the third, the fifth and the seventh.

If it is a grand banquet, the arrangement of tables should also be considered. The table of honor is placed in the front and center of the hall. The tables on the left are in turn the second, the fourth and the sixth and those on the right are the third, the fifth and the seventh. People take seats according to the identity, status and degree of relationship to the host.

Kung-fu Tea

Kung-fu tea was derived from the method recorded in The Classics of Tea written by Lu Yu of the Tang Dynasty (618-907), as one of the tea ceremonies popular in southern China, it combines spirit, ritual, brewing technique, art, and appreciation into one.

In this method, tea is brewed with spring water. When the water is boiling, put tea into a small pot and brew it with the boiling water, and then pour warm water over the pot. The specialty of this method is to heat the pot with warm water both inside and outside in order to bring out the best quality of the tea.

Tea sets used in Kung-fu tea are delicate, with special brewing techniques and drinking procedure. This ceremony is not only a pastime but also a social activity to promote friendship and greet guests. The tea set, small and exquisite, usually comprises a pot and three cups, sometimes two or four cups. As for the water, it is best to use spring or well water to brew the tea. Kung-fu tea requires a special tea named Oolong, such as Iron Kwan-yin, Asphodel, and Phoenix tea. Oolong is a kind of half-fermented tea, between green tea and black tea. Only this kind of tea has the special color, scent and flavor required by Kung-fu tea. Kung-fu tea is famous for its strong flavor that is too bitter for the first taste. But once one gets used to its strong taste, no other tea can compare.

Kung-fu Tea

Tea Pot

Kung-fu Tea ware

The standard Kung-fu ceremony tea requires some special technique. Generally, there are four people involved in one ceremony, including the brewer who handles the process. First boil water and put tea into the pot. Then pour the boiling water into the pot and scrape off the foam with the lid. Use the first brewing of tea to wash the cups with a purpose of creating a special atmosphere and making guests get the first touch of the tea spirit. After washing the cups, pour in the shrimp-palp water. Now, the tea has already brewed to a perfect state, and is ready to be served to guests. To be qualified a skillful brewer, the amount and color of the tea in the cups have to the same. The tea-offering order should go from the most distinguished guest to the guest on the left hand and then to the guest on the right hand and last to the host himself/herself.

Hotpot

Three or four buddies sitting around the table, watching the little spicy pot boiling slowly, with dozens kinds of meats and vegetables ready for you to cook them in the soup, that is the joy of having hotpot in China. Hotpot is called "huoguo"(火锅) in Chinese, which literally means "fire pot" because traditionally the pot was heated over a fire. Today, hotpot is often heated on an electrical stove or gas stove to avoid the smoke.

Sichuan Hotpot was recorded even in the Three Capitals Rhapsodies written by Zuo Si, a writer of the Jin Dynasty, which proves its history is at least 1,700 years. Originally from Sichuan, Southeast China, this particular cooking style refers to clay pot cooking, with varieties of ingredients placed into the pot and cooked on the table. Originally, it

Double Pot

Red Pot

was a seasonal food designed to protect against the low temperatures and frigid winds of winter (a saying goes like this: vegetables can serve as food while hot pepper kills cold). People would sit around a table, eat hotpot, and revel in the instant warmth that would flood their bodies.

Local people favor an oily-red broth that sets the eyes stinging, bubbling with onion, garlic and chili. Today Sichuan hotpots have increased in variety to include the "Red Pot" (Spicy hotpot flavor with beans and lobster sauce being basal materials), the "White Pot" (seafood hotpot flavor with bone broth) and "Double Pot".

Meats eaten in hotpots include lamb, chicken and beef that are usually sliced thinly for cooking. Meat or vegetables are added individually into the hot broth with chopsticks, and the cooking time is brief. Meat often only takes 15 to 30 seconds to cook.

Eating hot pot is a joyful experience. First, you need to choose the pot - spicy, pure or a combination of two - for the soup and dipping sauce. After the spiced soup boils with a hazy steam, fish, meat, bean curd and vegetables can be added. When the soup boils again, you can eat. Often people dip their food in a little bowl of special sauce before eating, but be careful, the soup is hot!

There are often disagreements between different hot pot enthusiasts. Some like to place items into the hot pot at a relaxed, leisurely pace, enjoying the cooking process, while others prefer to throw everything in at once and wait for the hotpot to return to a boil.

Chinese Families

The stereotyped view of the Chinese family is that of a large extended family, with several generations and immediate family all living under one roof, a self-sufficient institution for its members that provides childcare and the care of the elderly.

Traditionally, Chinese families were made up of those related by blood, marriage, or adoption, all living and managing their finances together. In the ideal family, three, four, or five generations all lived under one roof. The oldest competent male had ultimate authority in all family matters. Sons obediently follow their fathers' direction in choosing career and spouse. Every member of the family worked together for a single objective: sustaining and increasing the family's wealth and status. Such a large, multi-generational family can grow to be very complex.

A Chinese family

This picture no longer fits the modern Chinese family. The Chinese families now are usually small, consisting of a husband and wife living with their children and sometimes their parents. Only a small number of Chinese families live with or near large extended families.

However, the Chinese continue to emphasize the values of family, and to maintain close family relationships. There is a strong bond between parents, children and other family members. It is still customary that Chinese parents expect all their children to return home for the Chinese New Year Eve's dinner and other festival celebrations.

In the past, each Chinese family had a head, who had absolute authority at home, and had the final say in family affairs. But now in most Chinese families, the husband and wife, or a couple with other family members, make household plans together, and decide family affairs jointly.

Moreover, family members share the housework, making the division of labor at home more reasonable. When it comes to making a living, the husband and wife support each other's work.

Chinese people have the tradition of respecting the old and loving the young. Though many young couples do not live with their parents, they maintain close contact with them. Grown-up children have the duty to support and help their parents. The Chinese people attach great importance to relations between family members and relatives, and cherish their parents, children, brothers and sisters, uncles, aunts and other relatives.

Chinese Family Relationships and Titles

Traditionally, Chinese families consisted of many family members, up to three or four generations all living under the same roof. Males played the leading role in the family, and sons inherited their family names and family fortune from their fathers.

Family relationships are explicitly classified in a Chinese family, and each family member is granted a specific title. In China, the classification of familial relationships is primarily based on five elements: generation, age, lineal/collateral, male/female, paternal/maternal. As the called for in tradition, titles give respect to one's elders, who would never be simply addressed by name. Chinese familial titles also highlight the difference of paternal and maternal relatives.

For example, the titles of father's older brother, father's younger brother, mother's brothers, auntie's husbands are clearly distinguished in the Chinese language, whereas in English they are all called "uncle." In English, titles are more general, so "grandpa" may indicate your father's father or your mother's father, and your older and younger siblings could be easily confused if you don't specify age. All of these family members have their own titles in the Chinese language - even the titles of cousins indicate whether they are older or younger, male or female and paternally or maternally related. So in China, people know exactly who you are talking about as soon as you mention a particular relative.

A three-generation family

076

Chinese Family Structure and the One Child Policy

The traditional family in China consists of several generations all living together, and the family structure is shaped like a pyramid. Taking a three-generation family as an example, grandparents are at the top of the pyramid with a maximum of four family members, in the middle are parents and parents' brothers and sisters, and grandsons and granddaughters are located at the bottom level making up the most family members. The whole family is closely connected around the eldest generation, from top to bottom and elder to younger.

However the traditional family structure is now being turned on its head. Thanks to China's One Child Policy, enacted in 1978, the first

Parents and kids

An only-child family

generation born under the One Child Policy is now reaching the age of marriage and childbearing. Though most modern Chinese families try to keep the tradition of whole family living under the same roof, the traditional pyramid-shaped family structure has been reversed. Four grandparents, two parents and one child constitute the new model Chinese family, the "421 family".

Sociologists worry the 421 families will dilute family traditions and corrupt the traditional family roles, which were derived from thousands of years of history. People would have no brothers, sisters, uncles, aunties or cousins, and instead four ancestors would have only one descendant within three generations. Fortunately, the government has realized these problems, and has been working on solutions. To reduce the drawbacks of the One Child Policy, many measures have been put into effect, for example if a husband and wife are both only children, they can have two children.

077

Chinese Names

Usually a Chinese name consists of two parts, the family name first, and the given name second. So, the basketball player Yao Ming should be called "Mr. Yao", not "Mr. Ming". This is the opposite of the Western tradition of given name first, surname last. For thousands of years in China, the family name has been inherited from one's father. Chinese given names usually have one or two characters, but some minorities like to have really long names with up to 11 characters. Given names always express a kind of wish. Some names indicate the location, time or natural phenomenon of when the person was born, such as 京 (Beijing), 晨(morning),冬(winter), and 雪(snow). Some express the wish for great virtues, such as 忠(loyalty), 礼 (etiquette), and 信(faith). Boys' names usually have characters connoting power and vigor, such as 健 (health), 龙(dragon), 雄(grandeur), 伟(magnificence), 刚(strong). Girls' names usually use characters representing gentleness and beauty, 玉(jade), 彩(color), 雅(graceful) and 静(calmness), to name a few. Nowadays young people are more concerned with showing their personality, so they choose more flexible and fashionable names. Some people even add an English letter in!

The followings are some common names for boys and girls in China.

Boy's name	Girl's name
王伟	张丽
李健	王英
刘龙	张书雅
徐明	赵慧慧

078

How Do You Address People in China?

It's rare for Chinese people to address someone by their full name or given name unless they are close friends or immediate family members. When addressing people, it is common practice to use titles like Mr.(先生 Xiānsheng), Mrs.(夫人 Fūren) and Miss (小姐 Xiǎojiě). The title is placed after their name, thus Miss Zhao is Zhao Xiaojie in Chinese. The word Mister(先生 Xiānsheng) literally means "first born", which conveys the idea that anyone born before you is older than you, and thus deserves respect due to their age. On some occasions 先生 also means "teacher". Women do not change their family name when they get married. The Chinese also like to use words that express professional or social status when addressing each other or referring to other people. This underlines the fact that social roles and the status of individuals are very important, even defining how people relate to each other in China. The surname comes before the title, for example, Doctor Zhang(张大夫 Zhāng dàifu), Accountant Li(李会计 Lǐ kuàiji), Teacher Liu(刘老师 Liú lǎoshī), Principal Wang(王校长 Wáng xiàozhǎng), Mayor Zhou(周市长 Zhōu shìzhǎng) and so on.

Another interesting phenomenon is that people like to address non-relatives as if they are relatives to show respect. So when you hear about someone's "Aunty Liu", it certainly doesn't mean she is really an aunty, but may be one of his/her mother's good friends.

079

What do Chinese People Talk About When They Meet?

If you haven't been told "have you eaten" is as same as "hello" in China, maybe you are not ready for the next step in small talk. There are great differences between China and the West. Chinese people talk about more private things, such as personal health, family members, salary, marriage and age, topics which many Westerners view as private matters. However, by asking these questions, Chinese people show they really care about you. In the following Chinese conventions, you may find the cultural differences to be shocking.

1. In China, friends or neighbors often ask how much you paid for recently bought items or presents. In Western countries, this kind of questioning might be embarrassing, but in China it is completely acceptable.

2. When Chinese people greet someone who has traveled a long distance, they may show their sympathy by asking "I'm afraid you must have had a tiring journey" or "you must feel very tired." This is notably different from "did you have a good trip" or "did you enjoy your trip" in Western culture.

3. In China, the elderly are honored and given many privileges. Chinese people often ask an elder's age to show their respect. Westerners, however, may find this offensive because many dread growing old.

The Most Widely Used Greeting in China 吃了吗 (chī le ma)

Chinese people like to ask 吃了吗 which literally means "Have you eaten?" when they meet. At first, foreigners may feel confused about this, but slowly you will realize that they are not always asking you out to dinner, but are just asking as a greeting. This greeting has deep roots in china's agricultural history. In ancient times, the majority of people lived off of farming. The old Chinese saying 民以食为天 means "food is the staff of life." Commoners

Two elderly people greet each other in a park.

always worried about food and whether they would go hungry. That can somewhat explain why 吃了吗 means so much to common people. It was one of the most widely used greeting in the 1970s, but in fact it was used with some conditions, for example, people didn't ask a stranger 吃了吗 when they first met. The more people knew each other, the more they would use it as a greeting. As the society developed, 吃了吗 gradually lost its original meaning, and turned into a much informal and casual greeting between friends. Nowadays young people in China are more likely to say "hello" or "hi" when they meet. If they really ask 吃了吗, it could be because they want to go eat and are asking you to go with them.

081

Asking for Directions in China

Have you ever asked for directions in China and ended up confused, in the wrong place, or frustrated when people replied 那边 which means "over there".

It can be a challenge getting the right directions in China - and this is true whether you are asking in English or Mandarin.

Where to ask for directions in China?

1. The best place to ask for directions in China is a guidebook or Google, the next best place is a hotel.

2. Try not to leave home or your hotel without directions.

3. Take a bilingual Chinese and English map and learn helpful sentences, such as 我要去这儿.

4. Ask a reliable person such as a policeman or a college student.

When you get different information about the same place from different people, there are several possible reasons.

1. Some people don't know how to give clear directions, especially when they can't speak English. In this case, you need to point out the general direction on the map.

2. People who haven't heard of the place you're looking for will probably tell you it does not exist.

3. Chinese people like to use 东边(east), 西边(west), 南边(south) and 北边(north) to give you directions, which may make you more confused.

4. Chinese people really have a large and general sense of direction and distance. They'd like to tell you "it's not far" （不远）, however it may take you half an hour to get there.

082

Giving Thanks and Responding

There are some cultural differences of note between the Chinese and Westerners when expressing thanks and appropriate responses. "Thank you" is widely used in English to show gratitude in all cases, regardless of whether it is between friends, strangers, superiors and juniors, or family members. In fact, "Thank you" is uttered in English not only to show deep appreciation and sincere gratitude, but also to politely respond in many day-to-day exchanges. On many occasions, the Chinese say 有劳您了(yǒu láo nín le) which means "sorry for bothering you" or do not say anything and just smile or nod.

In Chinese, 谢谢 is not frequently used between intimate friends and family members because it may imply a certain distance between the addresser and the addressee. Foreign speakers may respond to "Thank you" by saying "You are welcome/ It's a pleasure/ My pleasure/ Not at all/ Don't mention it/ That's all right." Chinese people tend to say 这是我应该做的(Zhè shì wǒ yīng gāi zuò de), which literally means "it's my duty or part of my job." Also, foreigners tend to hear the phrase 不客气(Bú kè qi) quite often. This is the appropriate response to 谢谢 but does not quite mean "you're welcome." Rather, it translates more closely to "no need to be so polite."

It may baffle Westerners that Chinese people are always telling them to be less polite, however, it doesn't mean that Chinese people are less grateful or that etiquette is unimportant. Generally speaking, Chinese people strive for modesty and humility. It is impolite to be arrogant and brag about oneself or one's inner circle. The expression is most often used in the negative, as in 不客气(Bú kè qi), meaning "you shouldn't be so kind and polite to me" or "you're welcome" to show humility.

The Chinese Virtue of Modesty

The Chinese have always had the reputation of being a very gracious people. In particular, Chinese frequently compliment foreign friends on their language skills, knowledge of Chinese culture, professional accomplishments, and personal health. Curiously, however, Chinese are as loathe to accept a compliment as they are eager to give one. As many of Chinese have explained, this is a manifestation of the Chinese virtue of modesty.

When being complimented, a Westerner would readily accept the compliment by saying something like "Thank you" to show his/her appreciation of the praise, but a Chinese would try to deny the truth of the compliment. In this situation, both may think they are behaving properly, yet neither of them would think the other is being polite.

A very pointed joke involves a new Chinese learner, Mr. W, who attends a young Chinese couple's wedding. Know only his own Western cultural norms, Mr. W praises the bride, saying she looks very beautiful. The bridegroom thanks him immediately and replies in Chinese 哪里, 哪里(nǎ li nǎ li) a humble response to compliments that literally means where. Mr. W, feeling a little embarrassed that his compliment was unclear, thus said in his broken Chinese, "hair, eyes, ears and nose, everywhere is beautiful."

Usually Chinese people won't directly respond to a compliment such as "you look amazing on that dress" or "you are the best in your field." They usually respond with, "no, I really didn't do all that well. You are much too kind." This doesn't mean the compliment isn't appreciated, it just reflects the long and deep custom of being modest and humble. Now, however, as the Chinese society advances, close friends and young people are beginning to respond to praise in a more direct way, saying the familiar phrase, "Thank you".

084

Partings in China

Western and Chinese cultures have very different ways to deal with saying goodbye.

1. Difference in perspective

In Western societies, as an encounter winds down "I" perspective reasons for terminating the encounter are presented. Typical comments are associated with expressions of apology, such as "I'm afraid I must be off, I have to relieve the baby-sitter." In Chinese society, during the

Bow to each other—Chinese ancient way of saying "Hello"
Hold one fist by another hand—the Chinese ancient way of saying "Goodbye" and "Please"

closing phase of an encounter, people usually use "you" perspective reasons for ending the encounter. Such expressions include 你挺忙的, 我就不多打扰了(Nǐ tǐng máng de, wǒ jiù bù duō dǎ rǎo le), literally means "You are so busy, I can't bother you any longer," and 你一定累了, 早点休息吧，我要告辞了(Nǐ yí dìng lèi le, zǎo diǎn xiū xi ba, wǒ yào gào cí le) means "You must be very tired, I have to go."

2. Difference in rhythm

Chinese leave-taking is very short and quick. Western people tend to feel it is so abrupt that they are not prepared for it. English speakers often signal several times before leaving, saying things such as "I did enjoy our talk and the lovely dinner, but I must be going soon" or "thank you very much for asking me over. I hope we'll be able to get together again." They may also mention a wide range of common acquaintances, in expressions such as "say hello to Jack for me." With these words, they may stand up from their seats and begin to leave.

After Chinese people bid farewell to their hosts, there is usually a much longer period of seeing them off. For example, hosts will walk their guests to the door, or to the ground floor of their building, or even out to the street. Chinese people cherish this long and sincere parting process of guests leaving. They probably say 走好(zǒu hǎo), 慢走(màn zǒu), 再来啊(zài lái a) and so on, which can't be directly translated into English but more or less means "walk well", "walk slowly", or "come again". It does not conform to Western pleasantries, and may confuse people who are used to saying "Bye", "see you" and "take care".

Giving Gifts in China

As we all know, China is famed for its courtesy. So when you visit a new friend for the first time, you'd better prepare a gift for the host. Chinese people call this gift giving 送礼. Presents can be expensive or cheap but should always be useful - a greeting card may not be a suitable gift for a Chinese friend when you visit him at his house. Gifts can be collectibles, such as paintings and calligraphy works by famous people. You can also give rare and unique regional crafts as a gift. There is a Chinese idiom that says 千里送鹅毛，礼轻人意重, literally means "if someone comes from a thousand miles away to give you a feather, nothing matters but the thought behind the gift."

When you give a gift to the host, they will want show their modesty, so they will say 人来就好了，还带礼物干什么. It literally means "your presence has already make us greatly honored, why do you bother to give a gift?" In fact, they are happy about your gift. Friends, relatives and neighbors like to visit each other and give gifts at holidays. They consider it a great opportunity to enhance their relationship and friendship. The number of gifts you give is also significant. For example, it is considered luckier to give a pair of gifts because "good fortune always come in twos."

086

Mianzi

Mianzi, or face keeping, is an important feature of Chinese etiquette. It is so important that it can sometimes sweep a business or relationship aside. On the physical level, both Lian and Mian mean the physical "face". On the connotative level, Mianzi stands for prestige or reputation achieved through getting on well in life. Lian is the respect of the group for a man with a good moral reputation, the loss of which makes it impossible for a person to function properly within the community.

A statue depicting an elderly man of Qing Dynasty

Loss of Mianzi can bring shame or disgrace. It applies to all levels of Chinese society and even applies on a national level. When Chinese people feel that they have lost face, a series of actions will follow to regain it. For example, if you bluntly refuse someone for dinner, you'd better have a strong and convincing reason or your refusal means that you don't show respect or "give face" to them, which may hurt their personal dignity, in Chinese they call this "losing face".

Giving face

You may give face to someone by praising him in front of others, especially the people that he/she values, such as important customers or government officials. It could also be done through presentation of token gifts, or expressing your gratitude for what he/she has done on occasions where people important to the receiving parties are around.

Saving face

You may save someone's face by coming to his/her rescue by saying something to salvage an embarrassing situation.

Keeping face

You may keep someone's face by subtly doing something for him. For example, intentionally lose the golf game that you could easily win.

However, Mianzi is not hypocritical. It is an integral part of the Chinese culture that demands accountability to collectivity. It is also a means you must create and maintain harmonious relationships among people. Chinese place high value on personal dignity does not mean that you aren't sincere when you help someone save face. Rather, it reflects a culture that sees accountability as a virtue.

Tipping in China

In many countries around the world, it is customary for consumers of hospitality and other services to provide tips to their servers. But because of their different social backgrounds, social systems, ways of thinking, norms of behaviors and customs, people may have different attitudes toward tipping. Tipping is neither an international regulation, nor is it required, it is a social custom.

In China, tipping is very rare, there is no obligation to leave a tip and people don't usually expect one. Sometimes, tipping even could be vaguely insulting, as people may think "Why would you need to pay me more? It's my job! You don't think I normally give good service?" Most government-operated hotels and restaurants prohibit acceptance of tips.

Yet over the past year or so, some changes have been perceived in the way to leave tips in China. Perhaps this change is due to the recent influx of foreign visitors, or increased general awareness of bar and restaurant culture elsewhere in the world. Tipping is sometimes expected in some of the bigger hotels and by younger service personnel, especially in the more open cities. While it's not traditional, it can be a way of recognizing good service. People can tip a tour guide, a driver, a hotel bellboy or a restaurant waiter in recognition of services offered by them. This may encourage them to continue their good work.

088

Bargaining in China

In China, with the exception of some modern malls, stores and supermarkets, bargaining is normally acceptable in most small shops. In addition, in the marketplace many products don't have price tags, so vendors will come up with a price depending on the customer. Bargaining is expected, so shoppers have to be prepared to first be given a price many times higher than what the seller will actually accept for the product. Try bargaining every time you shop; you may get a great price reduction and enjoy the fun and pleasure of shopping.

Bargaining is a little time-consuming and sometimes troublesome, so be fully prepared is very necessary - however, there is no need to be nervous. First, you should visit many different shops and markets to get a general idea about the reasonable average price of the things you want to buy. In bargaining with the seller, stay relaxed and always polite. Be patient and unflappable to facilitate the bargaining process.

The shopkeeper often charges higher prices than the actual value of the goods. Try to reduce the price to half of the asking price, and then spend some time on further negotiation. Never express how much you like the things you want to buy, as the seller may use this information to jack up the price. Try to find out as many flaws as possible in the product. In response, the seller may reduce the asking price. You can also pretend to walk away. Generally, this skill works quite well in most shopping places. If the price proposed by the seller is still unacceptable and outside your budget, you can use the walk-away technique. Usually, you will be called back again, and the price you offer may be accepted by the shopkeeper.

The last but not the least, speaking some Chinese is very helpful. To overcome the language obstacles when communicating with the Chinese shopkeeper, you will benefit from learning some everyday

Two girls are shopping in a mall.

Chinese phrases. Make sure that you get the things you buy at prices you are satisfied with. You may even find you take pleasure in practicing the exciting art of bargaining.

089

Banking and Currency in China

China provides a wide range of banking facilities and money exchange services, which are available in many big cities. The central bank of the People's Republic of China is the People's Bank of China. The big four state-owned commercial banks are the Bank of China, the China Construction Bank, the Industrial and Commercial Bank of China and the Agricultural Bank of China. In addition to the big four state-owned commercial banks, there are smaller commercial banks. The largest ones in this group include the Bank of Communications, CITIC Industrial Bank, China Everbright Bank, Hua Xia Bank, China Minsheng Bank, Guangdong Development Bank, Shenzhen Development Bank, China Merchants Bank, Shanghai Pudong Development Bank and Fujian Industrial Bank. Most of banks mentioned above provide money exchange services, but the Bank of China is the official one with the most extensive network for foreign currency. ATMs in the larger cities such as Beijing, Shanghai, Guangzhou accept international cards marked with VISA, PLUS or MAESTRO.

Chinese currency is not widely available internationally and can hardly accepted outside China. But this phenomenon has been changing recently, and many Asian countries even some western countries are beginning to handle payments in Chinese currency. The bank notes of China's currency are called Renminbi

ATM

(RMB), also known as Yuan, and literally mean "The People's Currency." One Yuan equals 10 Jiao, one Jiao divides into 10 fen. Yuan is also called as Kuai and Jiao known as Mao in spoken Chinese. China's currency is issued in the following denominations: one, two, five, ten, twenty, fifty and one hundred Yuan; one, two and five Jiao; and one, two and five Fen. All par values have paper notes; the most common coins include 1 Yuan (Kuai), 5 Jiao(Mao), 1 Jiao(Mao). But Fen, the tiny denomination is rarely used now.

Chinese credit cards

100 yuan RMB

50 yuan RMB

20 yuan RMB

10 yuan RMB

5 yuan RMB

1 yuan RMB

Now the official exchange rate between the U.S. dollar and Renminbi yuan currently is about 1:6.80 (1 US dollar = 6.80 yuan RMB). The latest current exchange rate follows the currency market, changing every day.

090

Wangfujing

Situated just a few blocks east of the Forbidden City, starting with East Chang'an Avenue on the south and ending with China Art Gallery on the north, Wangfujing came into being more than 700 years ago. It was a favorite residential neighborhood of the rich and the royalty during the 17th and 20th century. It used to be the place where imperial brothers built their mansions. By the end of the 19th century, it was beginning to attract common residents and foreigners as well.

Today it is the busiest street in Beijing, 600,000 people come and go on the street every day, and on holidays, the number can rise to 1,200,000. The first famous business zone in Beijing houses a wide variety of shops and boutiques where you find all kinds of goods, some of which are of world-famous luxury brands. Apart from that, there are also many time honored stores with traditional goods that have stood in the street for hundreds of years. The Wangfujing Department Store has long been acknowledged as the largest, most fashionable, and best-known shopping

Xindongan Department Store (apm) on the Wangfujing Shopping Street

Pupils in class

years junior middle school, or six years of primary school plus three years of junior middle school). The government provides free primary education starting at age six or seven, then followed by secondary education. At this level, there are three-year or four-year junior middle schools, and three-year senior high schools. As a supplement to standard secondary education, students can choose vocational or technical secondary schools instead of senior high schools after they finished the compulsory education.

The increasing number of college-age students in China has already prompted one of the most remarkable expansions of education in modern times. Higher education is continuously growing, changing and developing. There are over 2,000 universities and colleges, with more than six million enrollments in total. China has set up a degree system, including Bachelors, Masters and Doctoral degrees that are open to foreign students. The country offers non-degree programs to foreigners as well.

New trends in Chinese higher education are attracting the attention of educators around the world. Since China began to develop a Western-oriented university model at the end of nineteenth century, Chinese higher education has continued to evolve. Since the late 1980s, however, tremendous economic development in China has stimulated reforms in higher education that have resulted in remarkable changes.

093

City Bus in Beijing

The Beijing bus system is one of the city's hidden treasures. Beijing buses are cheap, convenient and have a huge offering. Be prepared that most bus drivers do not speak English, and therefore it is advisable to have the name of your destination written in Chinese on a small piece of paper.

Beijing has a large, densely-woven network of public transportation. It operates so far a total of 708 routes with a fleet of 19,065 vehicles running between more than 4,000 stops scattered in downtown, urban and suburban areas of the city. Although having developed dramatically over the years, the public transportation system always seems a step behind the demands for more efficiency and comfort from commuters. Everyone has had the nightmare experience of being packed like sardines on a bus during rush hour, which is made worse every day by the increase in traffic jams.

On every bus there is a person whose main role is to sell tickets. However, a few bus lines don't have a person selling tickets, which is noted on bus windows. In these cases, passengers need to give the exact amount for a ticket, and cannot get change.

The Beijing bus system is quite complex, even more so when you are not fluent in Chinese. Once you are familiar with the bus system (this takes a while) the buses can bring you practically everywhere around Beijing.

A bus on Beijing's street

Bus inside

City public buses run from 5:30 a.m. till 23:00 daily, and can get very crowded during rush hours (6:30-9:00 and 17:00-19:00). There are different prices following the distance and the type of bus. Normal buses charge starting from only 1 yuan, if you buy a travelcard, it will give you a 60 percent discount, that is to say, 0.4 RMB every ride. Those equipped with air-conditioning or running on express lines are charged according to the distance you ride. Air-conditioned buses to the airport will charge around 16 yuan.

However, it's essential for you to know Chinese, because all signs along the bus routes are written in Chinese. If you can read Chinese, you can basically find a bus stop anywhere in the city, making it very easy to get where you're going.

094

Transportation in Beijing

Transportation options vary greatly in Beijing. Visitors can experience the most advanced and fast-developing modern transportation technology, yet they can also get a taste of the local and traditional Chinese rickshaw. Beijing has a complex network with subway systems, trains, buses, sightseeing buses and bicycles.

When travelling in Beijing, the best way to get around is subway. Beijing's subway serves 10 million passengers, with nine lines totaling more than 220 km and nearly 150 stations. Still, they are expanding. There are Line 1, Line 4, Line 5, Line 8, Line 10, Line 13 and the Airport Express (ABC), and still some lines are under construction. The current subway system is very easy to access. There is only one fare for tickets - 2 yuan RMB no matter how long you ride or how far you go. After the Beijing Summer Olympics Games, the automatic fare machines in subway stations became more popular for visitors. Only Chinese RMB can be used in the machines. The entrance turnstiles to the subway now use modern multiple-use cards or special tickets. Line 1 and Line 2 are always crowed, but very fast and punctual, and are a popular way to get to work.

Taxis are necessary for visitors in a new place. Most Beijing drivers can speak simple English like "hello" and "where are you going?" They are very

talkative and friendly. Although there still will be some language barriers and misunderstandings with the drivers, it is the most convenient way to get around. Taxi fares are comparatively cheap. Beijing taxis start at 10 yuan RMB for the first three kilometers, and add 2 yuan for each kilometer thereafter.

A station of Subway Line 2

A richshaw in the hutong

Biking through the streets of Beijing is my favorite way to see the city. You can cycle at a leisurely pace from sight to sight, stop for a local lunch, explore old alleys (hutongs) and become one with the Chinese in the bike lane. People chat as they cycle, carry oversized loads, and you'll even see arm-powered bicycle wheelchairs. Traffic jams will have little effect on you. During the 2008 Olympic Games, a bike was the ideal way to get around in Beijing.

Buses are heavily used in Beijing. Once you get used to the different types of buses and the routes, you can go anywhere in the city using a bus. This is the cheapest way to get around Beijing.

If you want to get a sense of old Beijing and some of the hutongs (alleyways), take a rickshaw. It is a great way to get a perspective of the local life. You can find rickshaws around some downtown areas and of course at most tourism spots.

Subway Line 13

095

Shanghai Magnetic Levitation Train

Several years ago the image was as alluring as it was futuristic - a train floating above its tracks races along at the speed of a jet plane. However, Shanghai bought into that dream in 2004. The city built the world's first commercial magnetic levitation train, named Shanghai Maglev Train. Construction began in March 2001, and public service commenced on 1 January 2004. During a test run on 12 November 2006, a maglev vehicle achieved a Chinese record speed of 501 km/h (311 mph).

The Shanghai Maglev was built to Transrapid specifications, which several other countries have been striving to use to create their own

A maglev train starts from Shanghai Pudong International Airport

The inside of Shanghai Maglev train station

Maglev trains. Ardently pursuing this goal is a German consortium, Transrapid. Germany has poured decades and billions of dollars into developing maglev technology, so has Japan done. Yet neither has put it to commercial use. The Shanghai Transrapid project took 10 billion RMB and two-and-a-half years to complete. The line is 30.5 km (19.0 miles) long and has a further separate track leading to a maintenance facility.

The line runs from Longyang Road station in Pudong, on the Shanghai subway line 2 to Pudong International Airport. The journey takes 7 minutes and 20 seconds to complete the distance of 30 km. A train can reach 350 km/h (220 mph) in 2 minutes, with the maximum normal operation speed of 431 km/h (268 mph) reached thereafter.

Following the opening, overall maglev train ridership levels were at 20 percent of capacity. The levels were attributed to limited operating hours, the short length of the line, high ticket prices and the comparatively inconvenient location of the Longyang Road terminus in Pudong, well away from the center of Shanghai.

This maglev train running between the rails with the locomotive, acting like a "free wheel", proved to be faster, quieter and smoother than wheeled mass transit systems and conducive to environmental protection; because of its electricity as a driving force, the train will not produce emissions, or pollution, and is a veritable green transport.

096

Qinghai-Tibet Railway

Qinghai-Tibet railway, the world's most highly elevated railway traveling across the "roof of the world," was dubbed a "railway to Heaven" as it is the highest "engineering marvel" that has linked Tibet with the rest of China. This railway is the first to connect China proper with the Tibet Autonomous Region, which due to its altitude and terrain is the last province-level entity in China to have a conventional railway.

The Qinghai-Tibet railway is 1,956 kilometers long, with 960 km of the track located 4,000 meters above the sea level and the highest point at 5,072 meters. It's the first time a railroad has entered the "forbidden zone for lives" on the Qinghai-Tibet route, with an average elevation of 4,000 meters above sea level. At the same time, the railway passes through China's largest uninhabited land.

Qinghai-Tibet Railway

A railway bridge across the Lhasa River

The railway boasts several world records. With an elevation of 5068.63 meters, Tanggula Station is the highest railway station in the world. Fenghuoshan Tunnel, with an elevation of 4905 meters, total length of 1338 meters, is considered to be the world's highest tunnel in a permafrost area. Kunlun Mountain Tunnel, 4648 meter in height, 1686 meters in length, is the world's longest tunnel in permafrost area. With a total length of 11.7 kilometers, Qingshui River Bridge is no doubt the longest railway bridge in permafrost area.

The Tanggula Railway Station is situated in the middle of the Qinghai-Tibet Plateau, 600 kilometers away from Lhasa. The location of the station was chosen at a place most suitable for passengers to view the Tanggula mountain scenery and take pictures. It is hoped that the Tanggula railway station will thus become one of the best scenic spots along the Qinghai-Tibet rail line.

There were and are many technical difficulties for such a railway. About half of the second section was built on barely permanent permafrost. Lack of oxygen is another problem in construction. Trains traveling across the roof of the world have extra oxygen pumped into the cabins to prevent passengers from suffering altitude sickness.

097

Beijing Capital International Airport Terminal 3

Beijing Capital International Airport Terminal 3 is ranked as a new design icon for the city of Beijing. This new terminal will set global standards for sustainability, operational efficiency and positive passenger experience.

The iconic terminal building, opened in 2008, is the world's largest airport building so far, and will provide what is already China's busiest airport with the extra capacity to service up to 90 million passengers annually. It is intended to be one of the most modern and passenger friendly super-hub facilities in the world, with clear and intuitive layouts, minimal changes of level, and fast transfer times.

Terminal 3 will also be one of the world's more environmentally sustainable airport buildings, and has been designed to accommodate Beijing's cold winters, hot summers, and short autumn and spring seasons. The terminal roof incorporates south-east orientated skylights

T-shaped terminal

The inside of Terminal 3

which enable the sun to warm the building on winter mornings, and make the most of available daylight during normal operational times. This gives dramatic reductions in the amount of energy needed for both heating and cooling.

In the center of the building you are quite far from the nearest wall, so you need to bring natural light in from the roof. Sunlight also warms the air, which minimizes the heating load. However, the proportion of the roof area that is glazed remains fairly low, so the building does not require a lot of cooling in the summer. The energy saving characteristics of the roof lights are another trademark honed during previous airport projects.

The entrance to the terminal reaches out into the surrounding landscape, as if to invite passengers arriving via the road and rail links into the building. The designer took a Feng Shui expert's advice on the shape of the arrival area, which is inviting and makes people feel very calm.

Shenzhou 7 Spacecraft

Shenzhou 7 (神舟七号) was the third human spaceflight mission of the Chinese space program. Shenzhou literally translates to Divine Ship, God Vessel, or Magic Vessel. The mission, which included an extravehicular activity (EVA) carried out by crewmembers Zhai Zhigang and Liu Boming, marked the commencement of the second phase of the Chinese government's Project 921.

Shenzhou 7 was the first Chinese space mission to carry a three-person crew for several days and conduct a full operation. On September 27, 2008, Zhai Zhigang, wearing a Chinese-developed Feitian space suit, conducted a 20-minute space walk, the first ever for a Chinese astronaut.

On September 25th, 2008, the Shenzhou spacecraft carrying the three crewmembers was launched, by a Long March 2F (CZ-2F) rocket which lifted off from the Jiuquan Satellite Launch Center at 21:10 CST. The mission lasted three days, after which the craft landed safely

Shenzhou 7 manned spacecraft was launched in Jiuquan Satellite Launch Center on Sept. 25th, 2008.

Shenzhou 3 Spacecraft

in Siziwang Banner in central Inner Mongolia on September 28, 2008, at 17:37 CST. The EVA carried out during the flight makes China the third country to have conducted an EVA, after the Soviet Union and the United States.

China impressed the world again by launching the Shenzhou 7 spacecraft into space and accomplishing its maiden space walk. The feat has made China the third country in the world to stage extra-vehicular activity and the only developing country capable of manned space exploration.

The Chinese Shenzhou manned spacecraft resembled the Russian Soyuz spacecraft, but was of larger size and all-new construction. Like the Soyuz, it consisted of a forward orbital module, a re-entry capsule, and an aft service module. Unlike the Soyuz, the orbital module was equipped with its own propulsion, solar power, and control systems, allowing autonomous flight. Shenzhou can be used to develop manned spaceflight techniques (extravehicular activity, rendezvous and docking) and later serve as a ferry to Chinese space stations. Like Soyuz, derivatives could be used as a lunar orbital and landing spacecraft.

The Shenzhou project received limited funding, resulting in a protracted development program which began in 1992. Shenzhou I was launched in 1999. It was China's first test spaceship. After completing a 12 hour flight and carrying out all the planned scientific experiments, the spaceship landed successfully in central Inner Mongolia.

Two years later, China launched Shenzhou II, which was the country's first unmanned spacecraft. Technically, it was almost the same as a manned spacecraft. It returned to earth seven days later. Experiments were carried out under minor gravity. Equipment functioned well and much scientific data was gathered.

In 2002, Shenzhou III was launched. Its design was the same as a manned spaceship. The craft travelled in space for seven days. Many experiments were carried out onboard. And during this flight, an emergency escape system was tested, with satisfactory results. This laid a strong foundation for the later development of a manned space mission.

Later in the 2002, China launched the Shenzhou IV spaceship. The craft was launched at a temperature of 18.4 degrees Fahrenheit, which set a new record. During its seven days in space, the spacecraft opened solar panels, adjusted its positions and realized orbital changes. After finishing all planned experiments, the spacecraft safely returned to Earth.

The first manned spacecraft was launched in 2003, with China's first astronaut, Yang Liwei, on board. The craft traveled in space for 21 hours and orbited the Earth for 14 times. It landed successfully in Inner Mongolia the next day. China became the world's third country to carry out an independent manned space mission.

In 2005, Shenzhou VI was launched with two astronauts on board, Fei Junlong and Nie Haisheng. During the flight, Chinese astronauts took off their suits for the first time and conducted activities and experiments on board. It was also the first time that people participated in space experiments.

Five days later, the space craft returned to Earth. Its mission meant that the dream of a manned space mission had become reality for China - for a second time.

099

The Giant Panda

While the dragon has historically served as China's national emblem, in recent decades the Giant Panda has become a symbol of the country. Its image is a public favorite, at least in part because many people adore its baby-faced cuteness. It is also usually depicted reclining peacefully eating bamboo, as opposed to hunting, which adds to its image of innocence.

The Giant Panda, commonly called the panda bear, is easily recognized by its comical face, large size, and its distinctive black patches around the eyes, over the ears, and across its round body. Though scientifically it is classified as a carnivore, the Giant Panda has a diet that is 99 percent bamboo. The Giant Panda eats other foods such as honey, eggs, fish, yams, shrub leaves, carrots, oranges, and bananas when available.

Lovely panda

The Giant Panda lives in the mountain ranges of only few provinces of central China, including Sichuan, Shaanxi and Gansu provinces. It once lived in lowland areas, but farming, forest clearing, and other development now restrict the Giant Panda to the mountains.

The Giant Pandas

    The Giant Panda is an endangered species and is highly threatened. According to the latest report, China has only 239 Giant Pandas in captivity and another 27 living outside the country. It's also estimated that around 1,590 pandas are currently living in the wild. Though some reports show that the numbers of wild pandas are on the rise, the International Union for Conservation of Nature believes there is not yet enough certainty to remove the Giant Panda from the endangered animal list.

100

The Beijing 2008 Olympic Games

The 2008 Summer Olympic Games was a major international multi-sport event that took place in Beijing, China. The Beijing Olympiad drew a record number of 204 sports delegations that cover the widest-ever geographical areas in the Games' history. This has enabled the world to see not only a "truly exceptional" Olympiad, but also a more open and colorful China. The Games saw 43 new world records and 132 new Olympic records set. A record 87 countries won medals during the Games.

On August 8, the Beijing Olympiad captivated some 2 billion spectators and TV audience members worldwide with its splendid opening ceremony, enabling them to enjoy a charming night that epitomizes China's 5,000-year civilization.

Firework display on the opening ceremony of Beijing 2008 Olympic Games

. At the start of the evening, 2,008 drummers welcomed the audience with a saying from Confucius, "Friends have come from afar, how happy we are!" Similar uniquely Chinese elements appeared throughout the performance. In one, a vast scroll unfolded across the stadium's floor. Projections of cliff paintings, pottery and bronze work dissolved into an ink-and-wash painting as a performance group dressed in black to represent ink on paper moved across the giant scroll. The ceremony combined state-of-the-art technology with strong images from Chinese myths, history and civilization, ranging from ancient Chinese characters and ink paintings to computer keyboards and astronauts.

A total of an estimated US$42 billion were spent on the 2008 Olympic Games in Beijing, making it the most expensive games ever. Its largest architectural pieces are the Beijing National Stadium, Beijing National Indoor Stadium, Beijing National Aquatics Center, Olympic Green Convention Center, Olympic Green, and Beijing Wukesong Culture & Sports Center.

A little girl is joyfully waving a flag with 2008 Olympic Games logo. To host the Olympic Games is a long-cherished dream of the Chinese people.

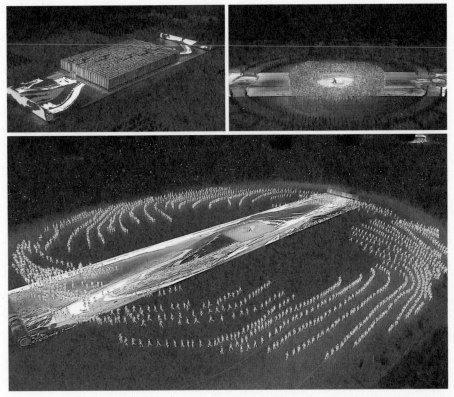

The Opening Ceremony of Beijing 2008 Olympic Games

To prepare for Olympic visitors, Beijing's transportation infrastructure was expanded significantly. Beijing's airport underwent a major expansion, adding the new Terminal 3, the world's largest airport terminal building so far, designed by renowned architect Norman Foster. On August 1, 2008, Beijing south railway station was reopened after two years of construction.

图书在版编目（CIP）数据

发现中国：英文 / 本书编委会编.—北京：五洲传播出版社，2009.9
ISBN 978-7-5085-1631-8
Ⅰ.发 … Ⅱ.本… Ⅲ.①汉语–对外汉语教学–语言读物
②中国–概况–英 Ⅳ.H195.5 K92

中国版本图书馆CIP数据核字（2009）第157308号

DISCOVER CHINA

出版发行：五洲传播出版社
地址：北京市海淀区北小马厂6号华天大厦24层
邮编：100038
电话：(86-10) 58891280/58880274
网址：www.cicc.org.cn

开本：165mm×240mm 1/16
印张：15
版次：2009年9月第一版第一次印刷
印刷：北京正合鼎业印刷有限公司
书号：ISBN 978-7-5085-1631-8
定价：85.00元